AF267478

INTRO

WELCOME TO THE BLACK BOOK CLUB : STRUCTURE OF GRAFFITI ART, AN ADULT COLORING BOOK DESIGNED FOR THOSE WHO APPRECIATE THE VIBRANT WORLD OF STREET ART. WITH 170 PAGES, THIS BOOK OFFERS A UNIQUE OPPORTUNITY TO EXPLORE AND ENGAGE WITH GRAFFITI THROUGH COLORING. EACH FEATURED IMAGE INCLUDES TWO COPIES, GIVING YOU THE FREEDOM TO EXPERIMENT WITH COLORS AND TECHNIQUES.

INSIDE, YOU'LL FIND FINISHED PIECES FROM ARTIST STUART AVORY, SHOWCASING THE MINIMALISTIC OUTLINES THAT DEFINE GRAFFITI ART. AT THE BACK, WE'VE INCLUDED A BRIEF TUTORIAL TO HELP YOU GET STARTED, ALONG WITH EXTRA PAGES FOR YOU TO CREATE YOUR OWN DESIGNS. THIS BOOK IS INTENDED FOR THOSE WHO WANT TO GAIN A DEEPER UNDERSTANDING OF GRAFFITI AS AN ART FORM, AND FOR THOSE WHO WISH TO PRACTICE AND DEVELOP THEIR SKILLS. IT'S AN OPPORTUNITY TO EXPLORE THE PROCESS, LEARN NEW TECHNIQUES, AND CREATE YOUR OWN WORK.

ABOUT THE ARTIST

SKUBAZ99

STUART AVORY IS A BLACKBOOK GRAFFITI ARTIST FROM THE LONDON AREA, RECOGNIZED FOR HIS WORK IN THE LATE 80S AND EARLY 90S. AFTER A LENGTHY HIATUS, HE RESUMED BLACKBOOK GRAFFITI IN 2022 AS A REGULAR HOBBY. YOU CAN FIND MORE OF HIS ART, ALONG WITH WORKS FROM MANY OTHER GRAFFITI ARTISTS, IN THE FACEBOOK GROUPS "GRAFFITI WARS" AND "GRAFITI SKETCHES."

MATERIALS

OPAQUE & FULL COVERAGE MARKERS:

1. POSCA PAINT MARKERS
   - Known for vibrant, opaque color. Great for smooth coverage.
   - Recommended sizes: 0.7mm, 3mm, 8mm.
2. MOLOTOW ONE4ALL ACRYLIC MARKERS
   - Excellent opacity and coverage. Ideal for both detailed and large areas.
   - Recommended sizes: 1mm, 2mm, 4mm.
3. KURETAKE ZIG PAINTY MARKERS
   - Smooth, opaque markers that provide clean lines and bold fills.
   - Recommended sizes: Medium (1.5mm), Broad (3mm).

BLACK PENS:

1. MICRON PIGMA PENS
   - Archival ink, perfect for precise line work and outlining.
   - Recommended sizes: 0.25mm, 0.5mm, 1.0mm.
2. UNI-BALL VISION ELITE ROLLERBALL PEN
   - Smooth and waterproof, great for bold outlines and fine details.
   - Recommended size: 0.5mm or 0.7mm.
3. STAEDTLER PIGMENT LINERS
   - Durable, waterproof ink, ideal for mixed media and detailed lines.
   - Recommended sizes: 0.3mm, 0.5mm, 0.7mm.

WHITE HIGHLIGHTERS:

1. UNI-BALL SIGNO BROAD WHITE GEL PEN
   - Opaque white ink for highlights and details.
   - Recommended size: 1.0mm.
2. SAKURA GELLY ROLL WHITE GEL PEN
   - Great for fine white details and highlights over colored areas.
   - Recommended size: 0.8mm or 1.0mm.

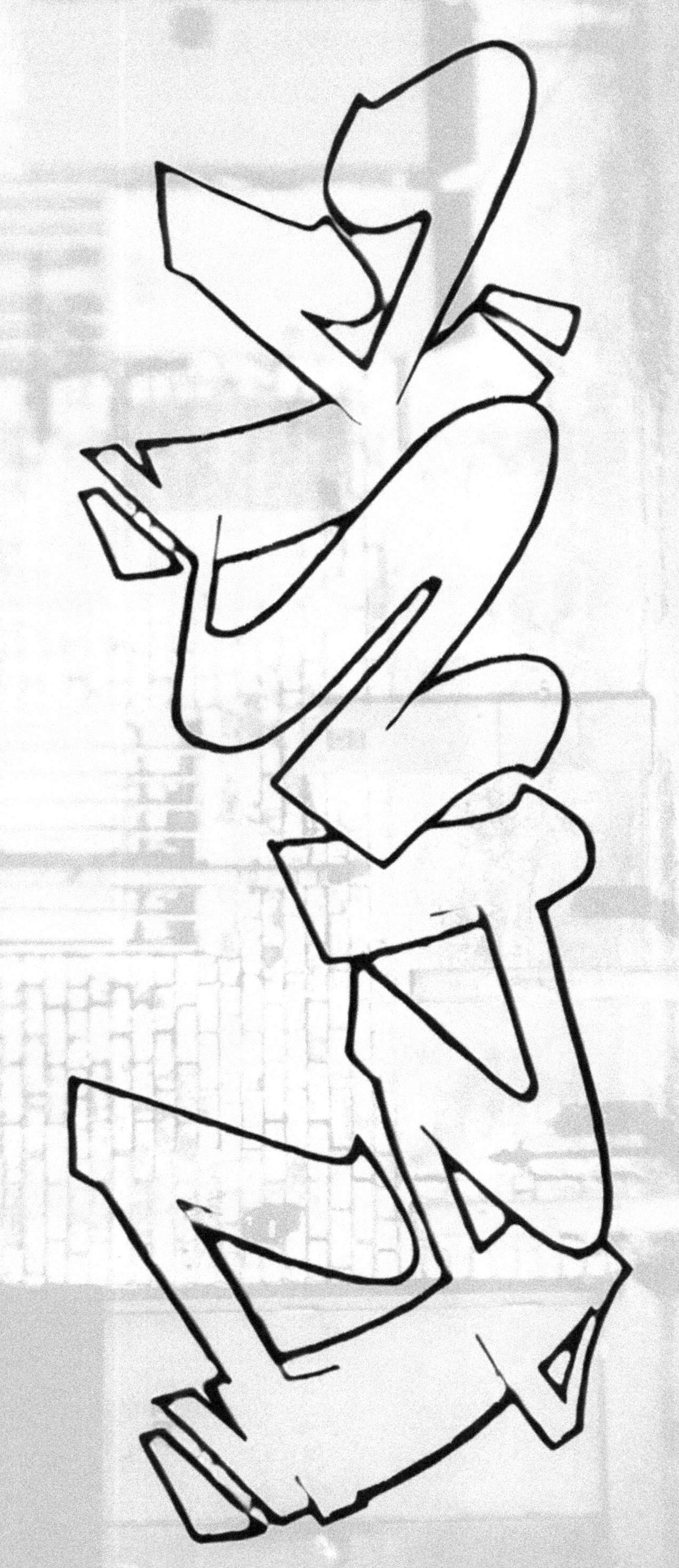

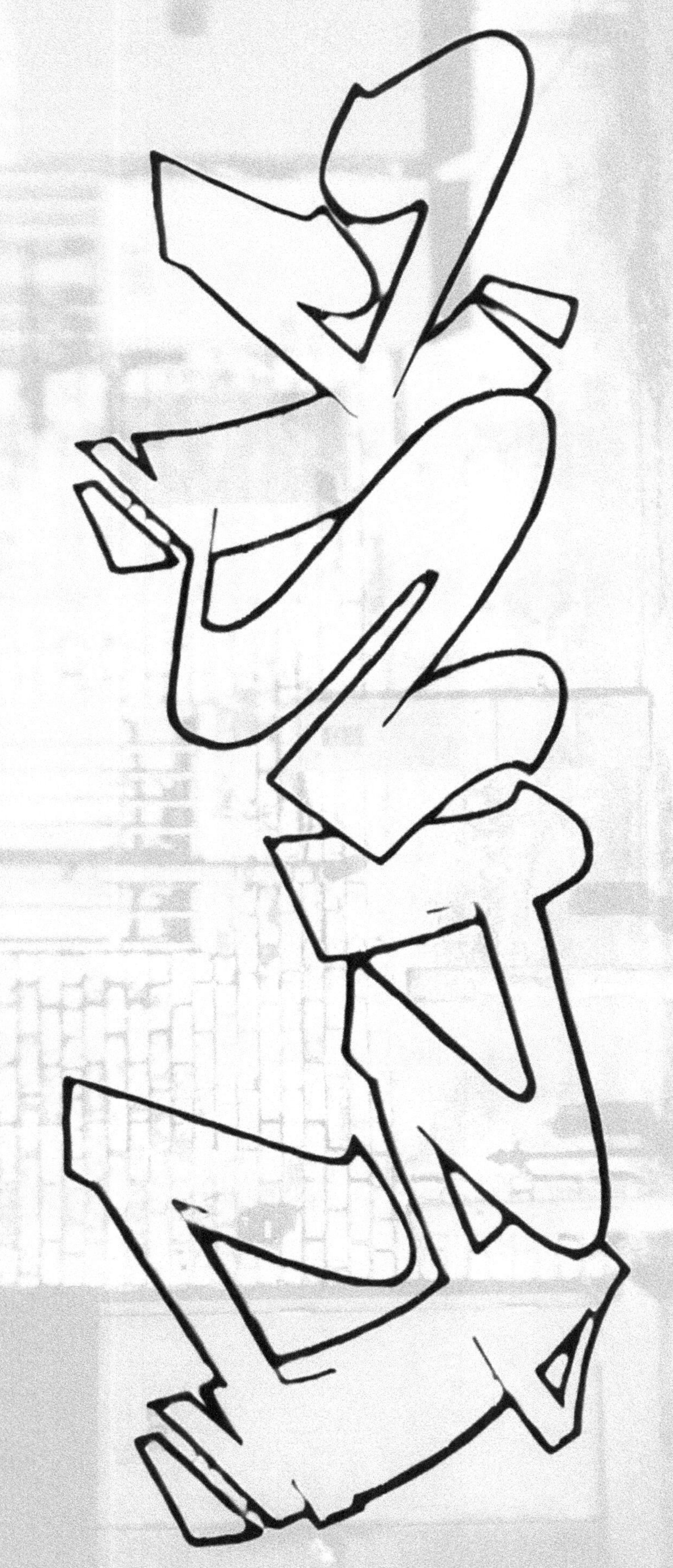

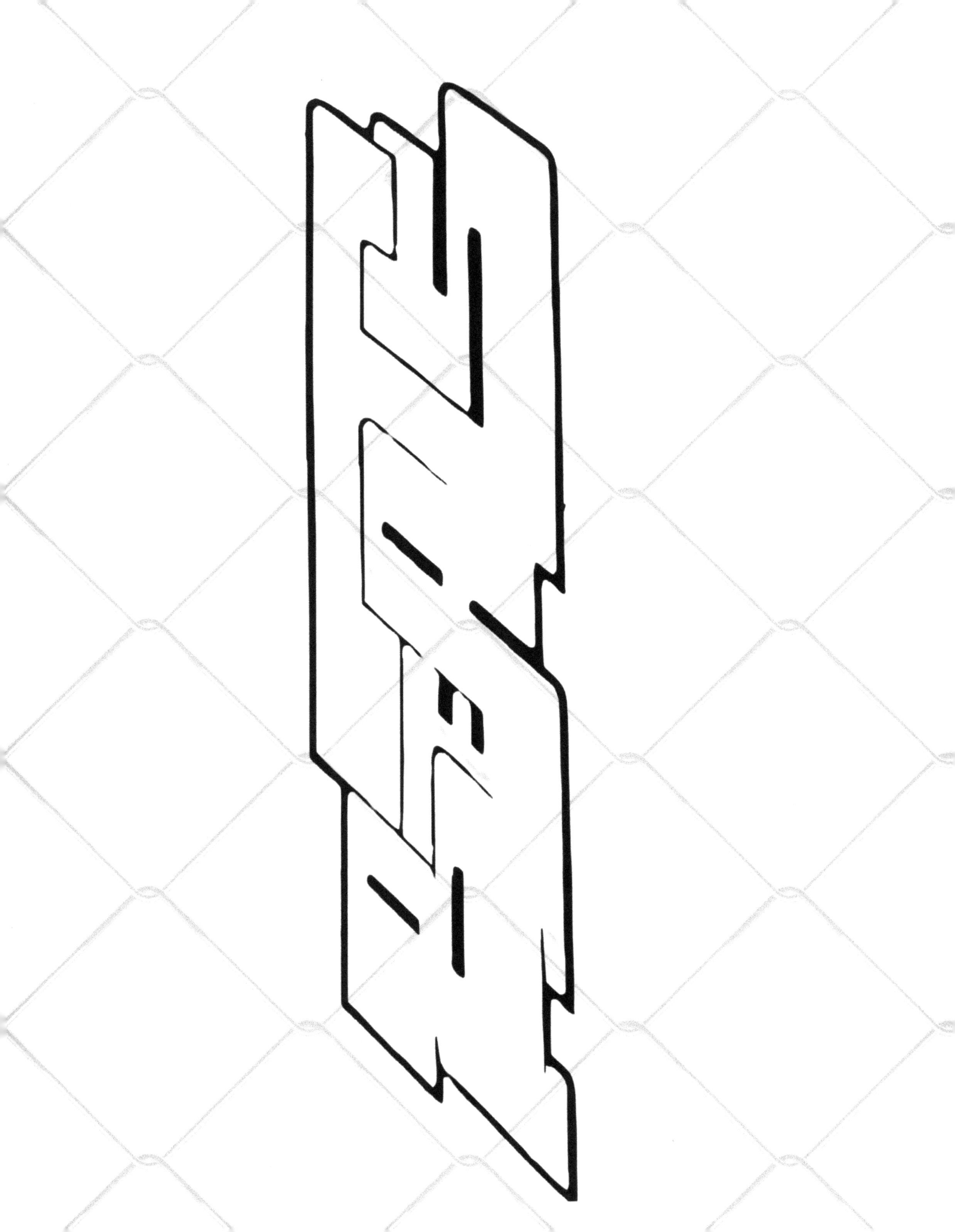

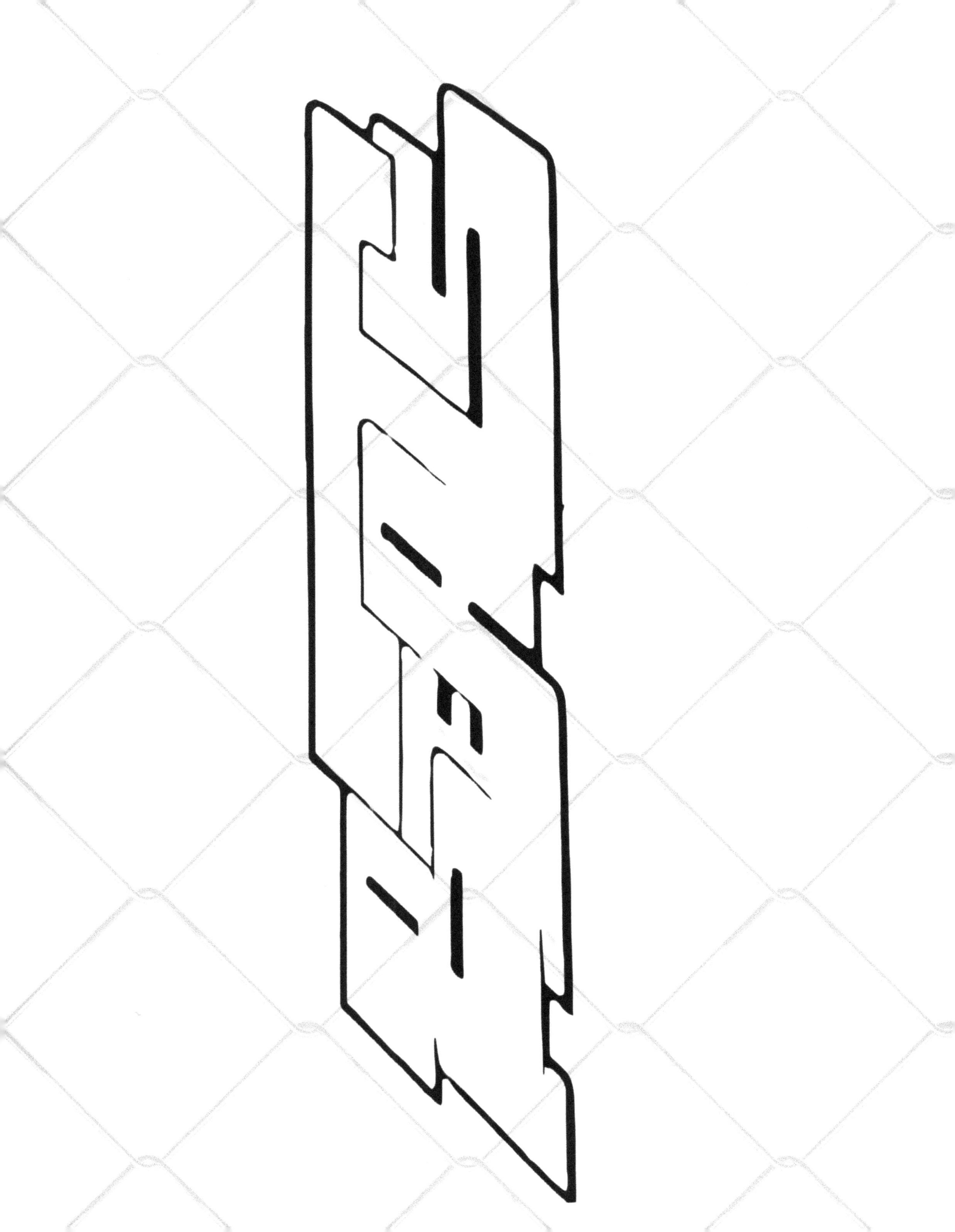

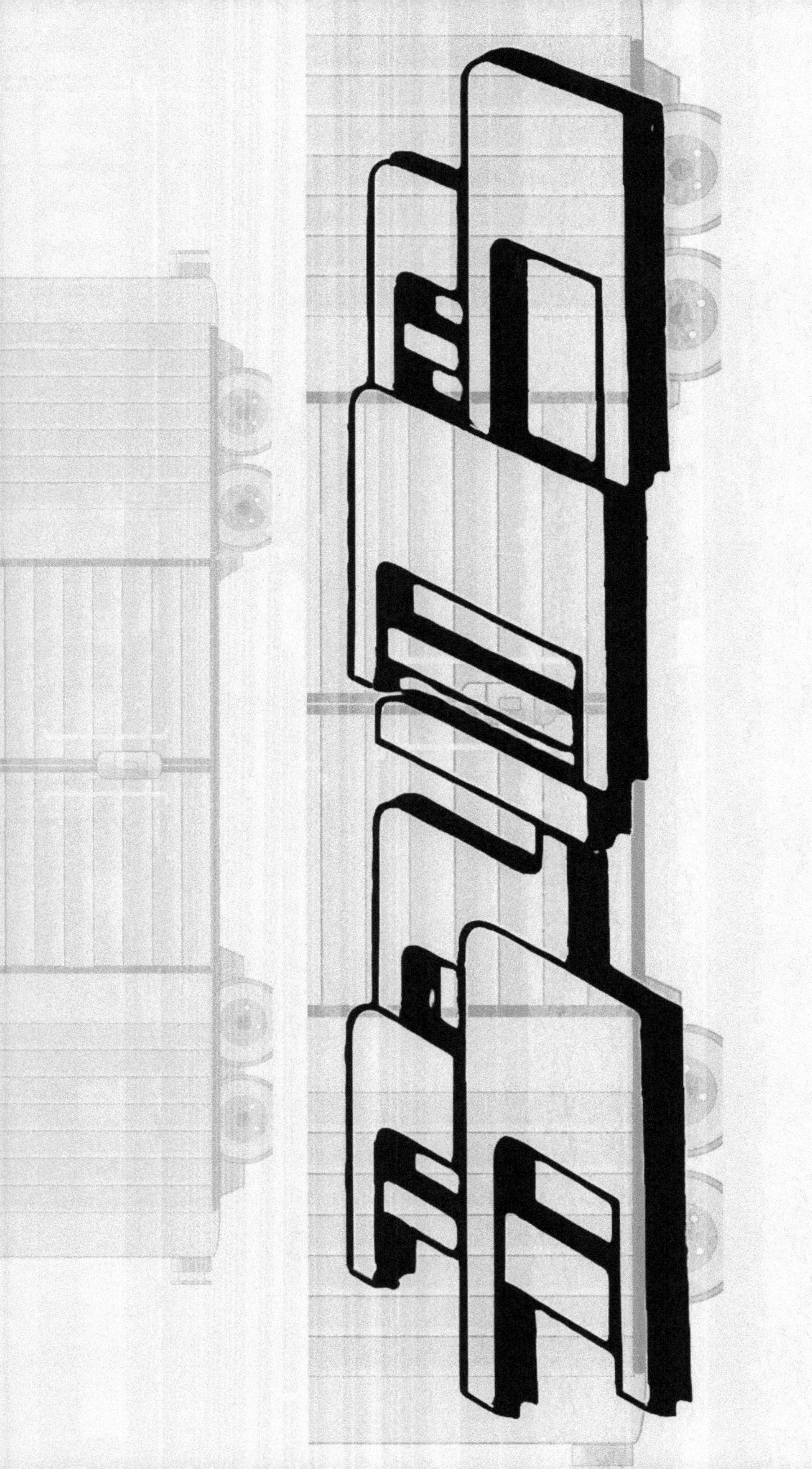

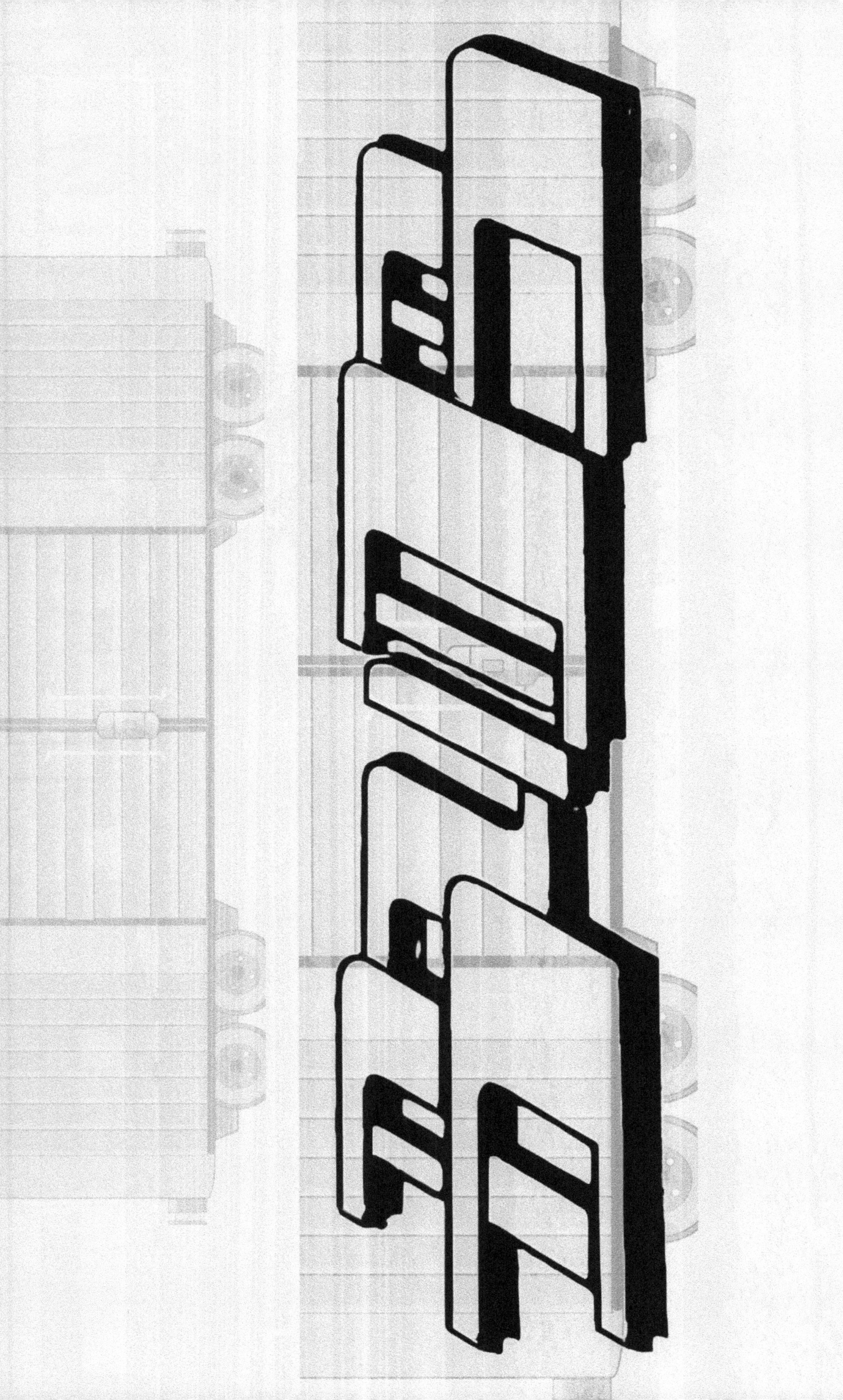

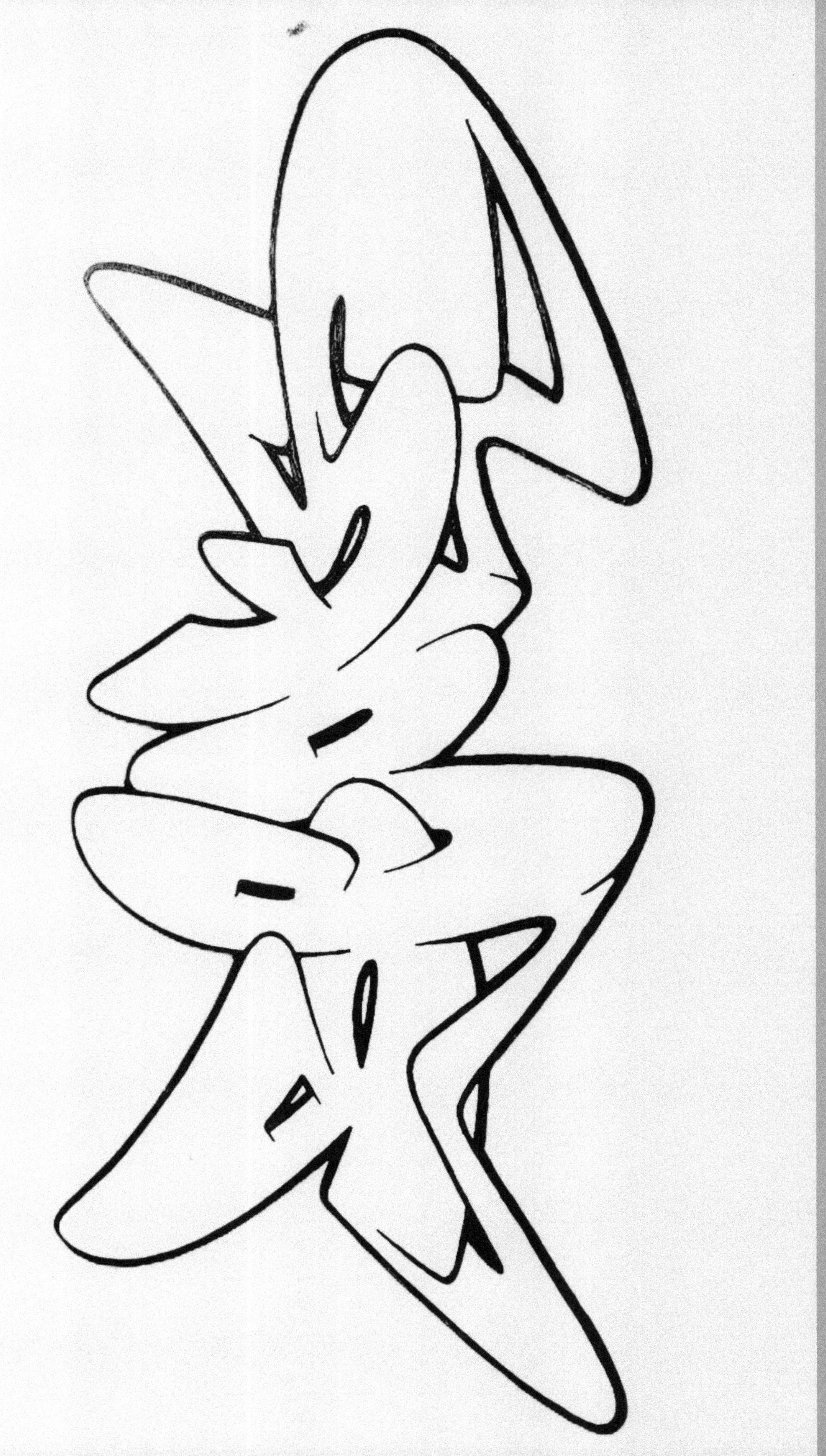

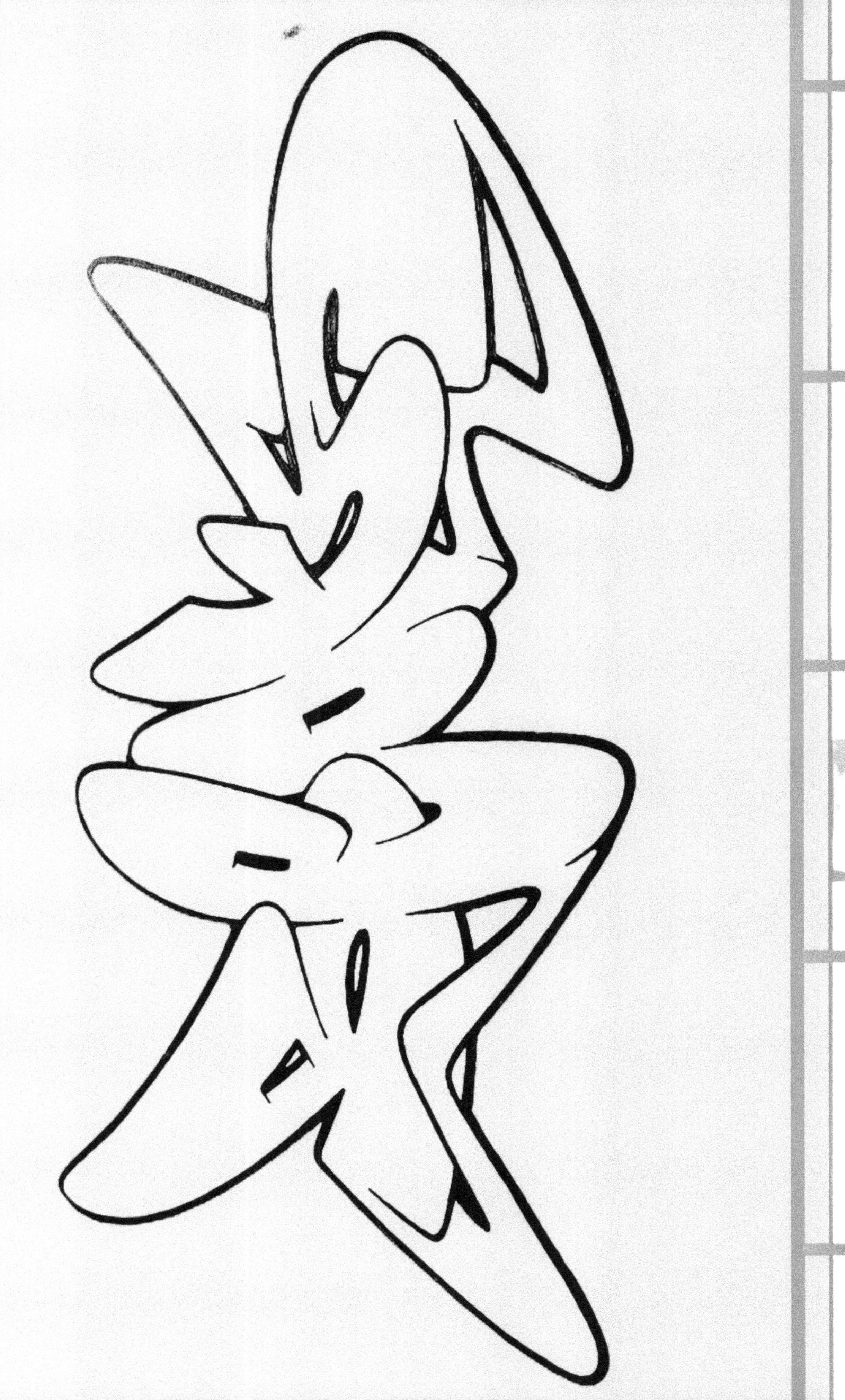

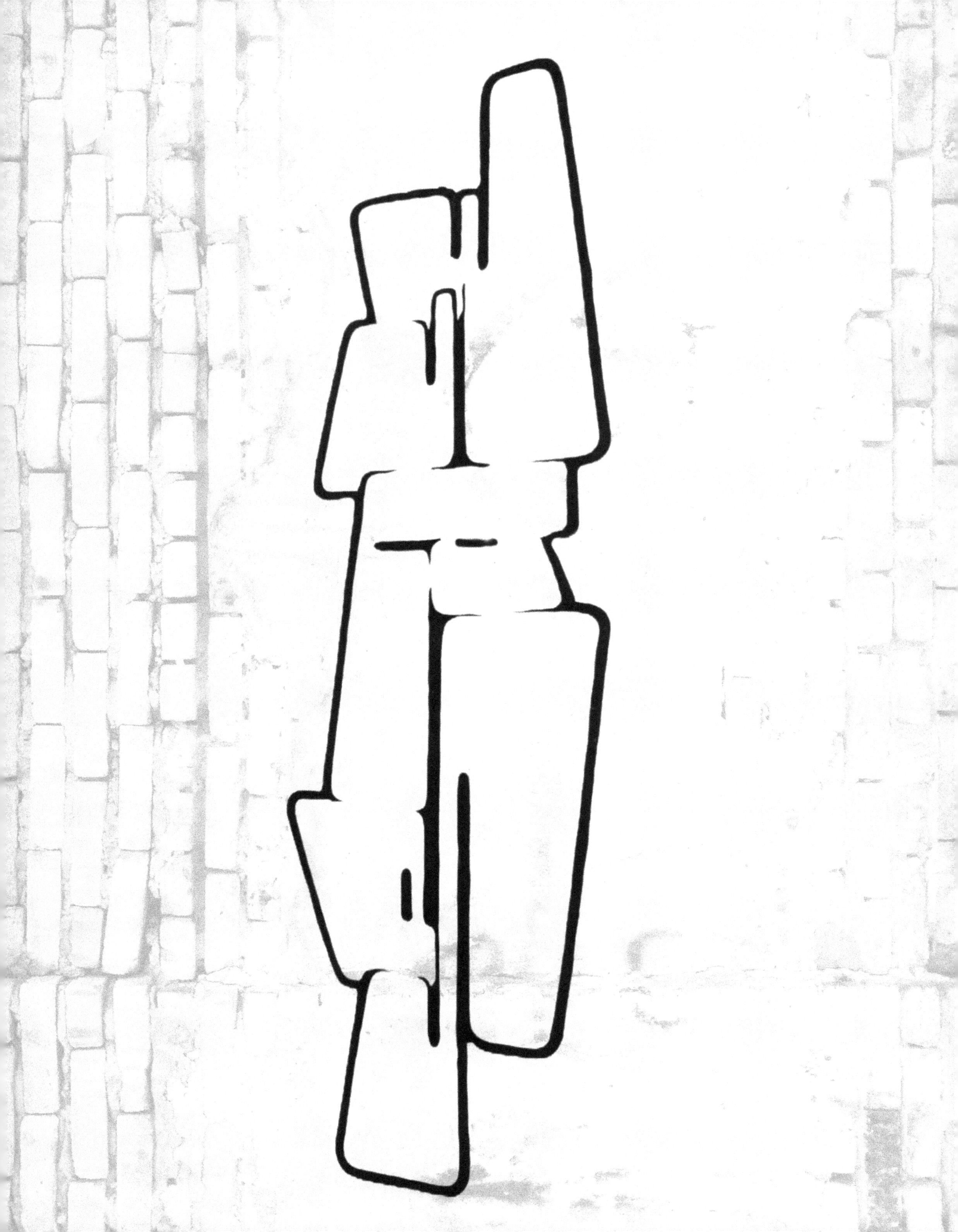

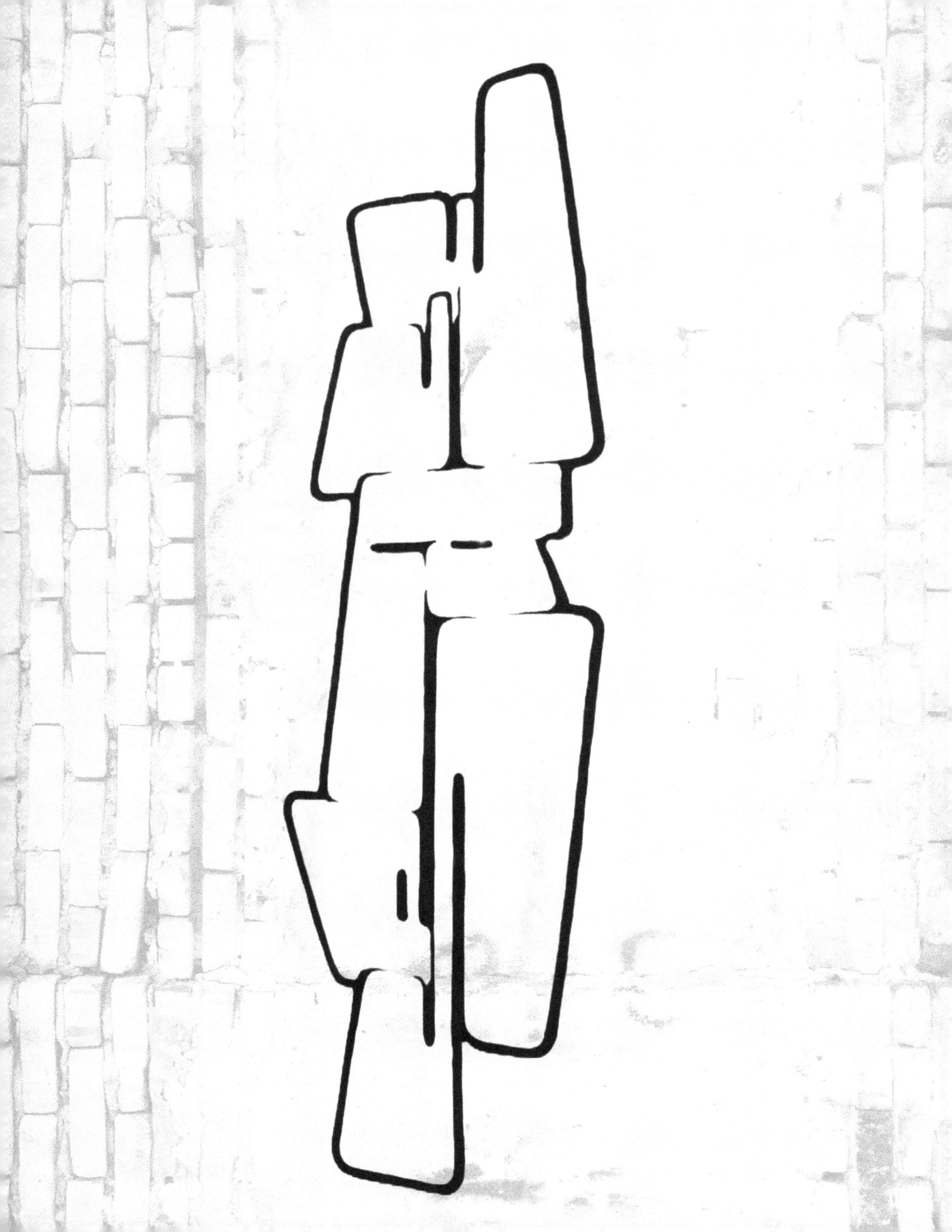

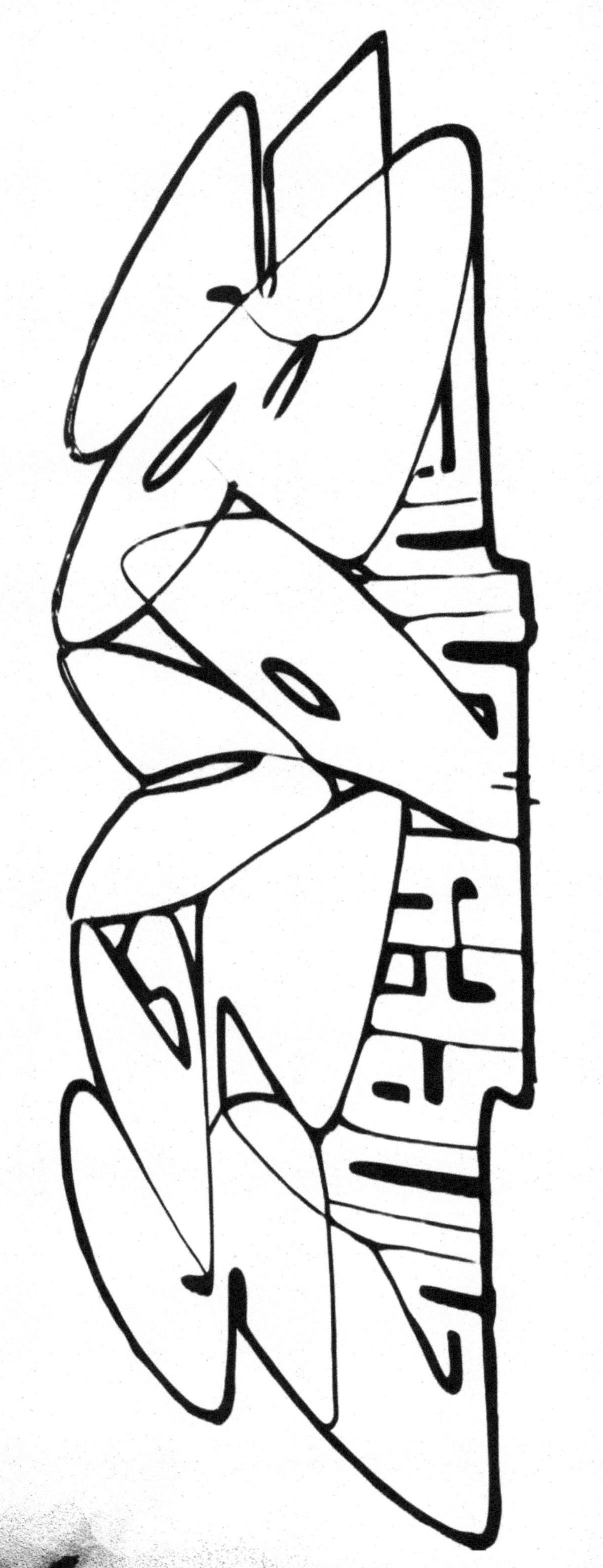

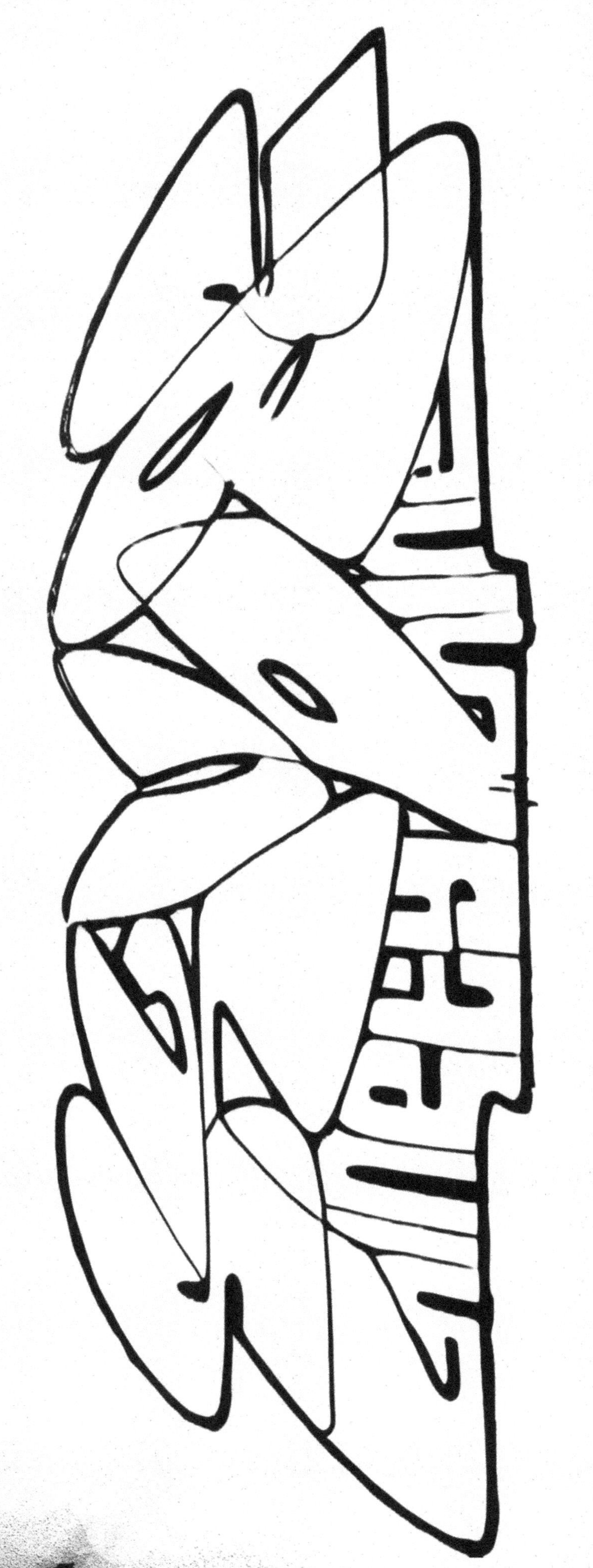

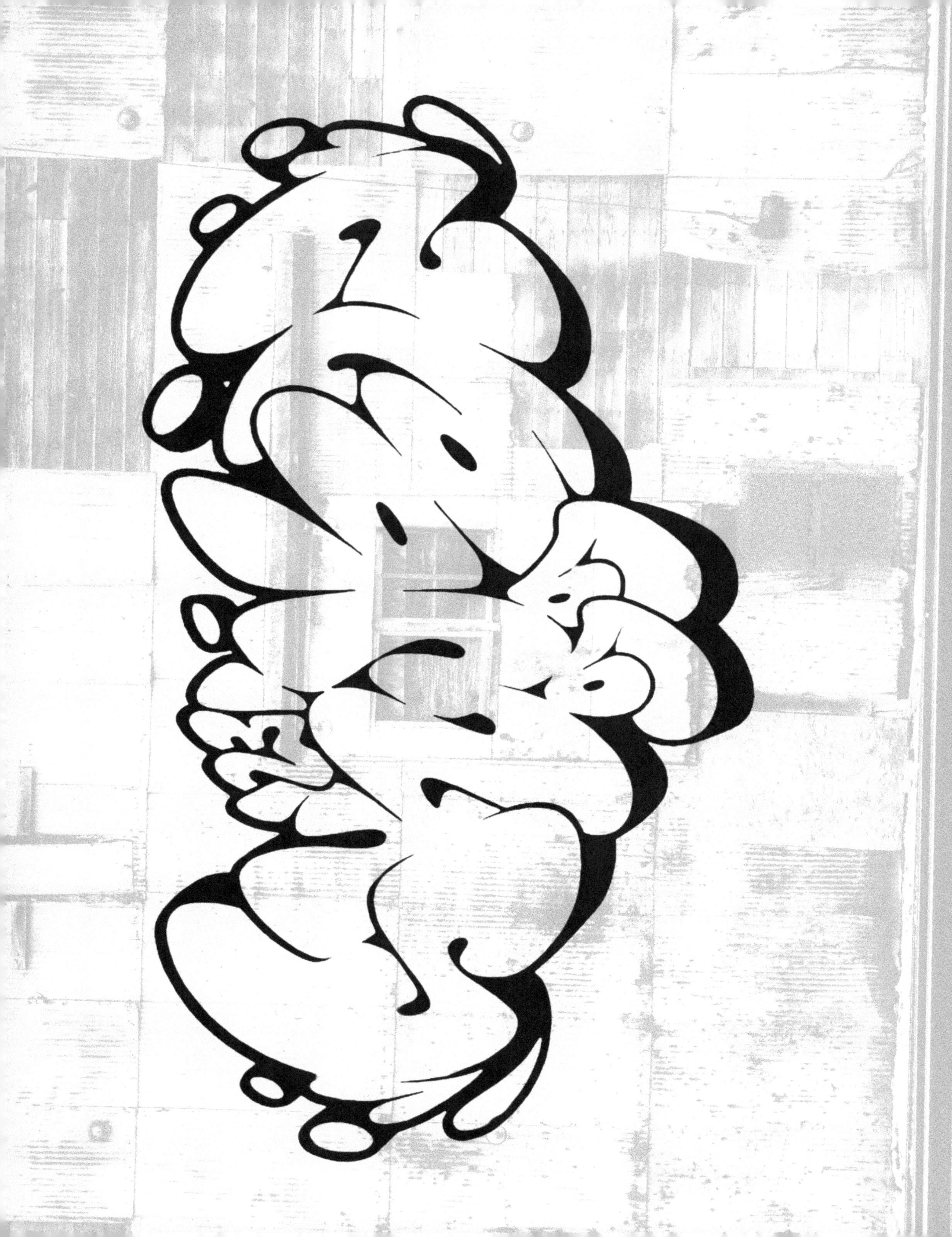

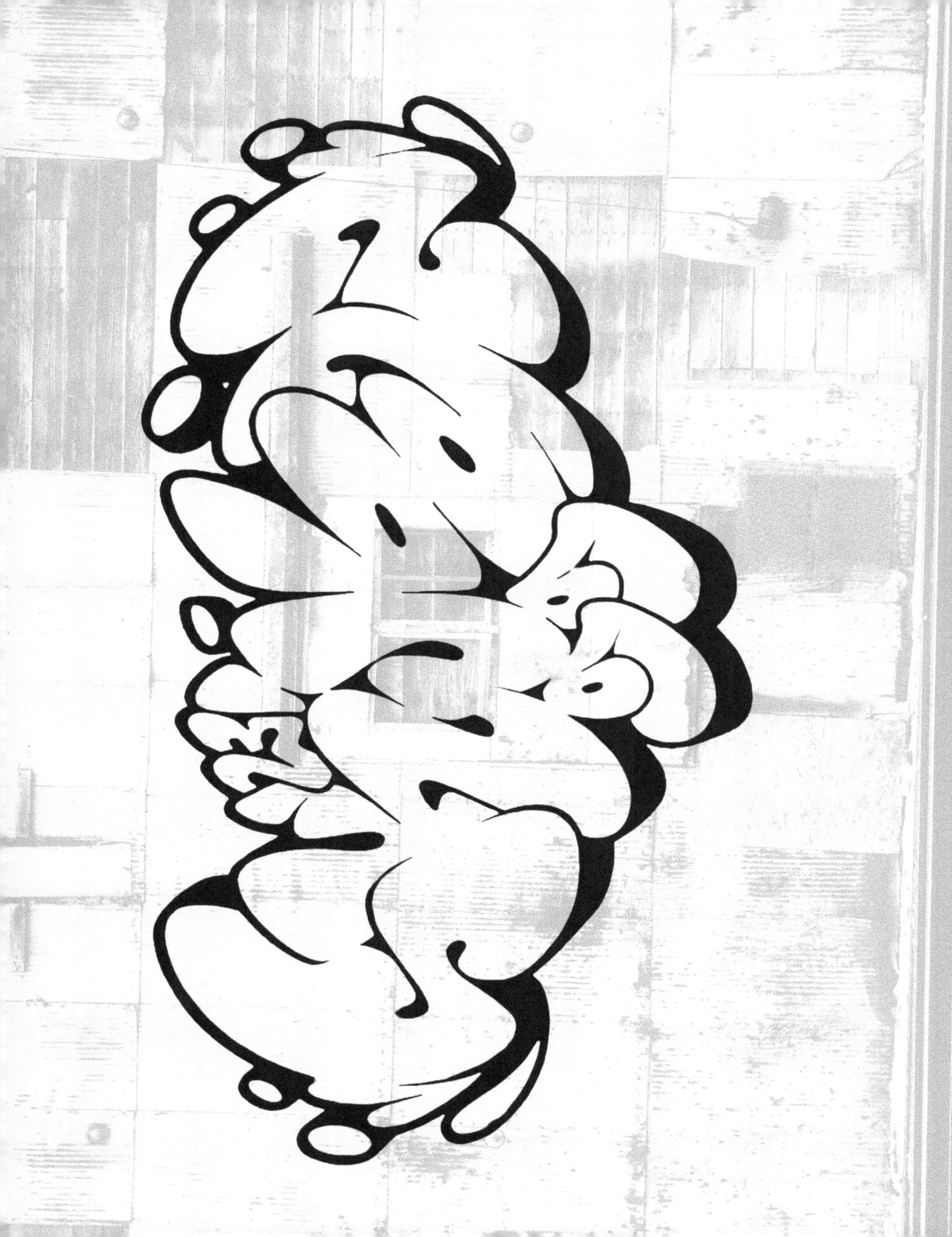

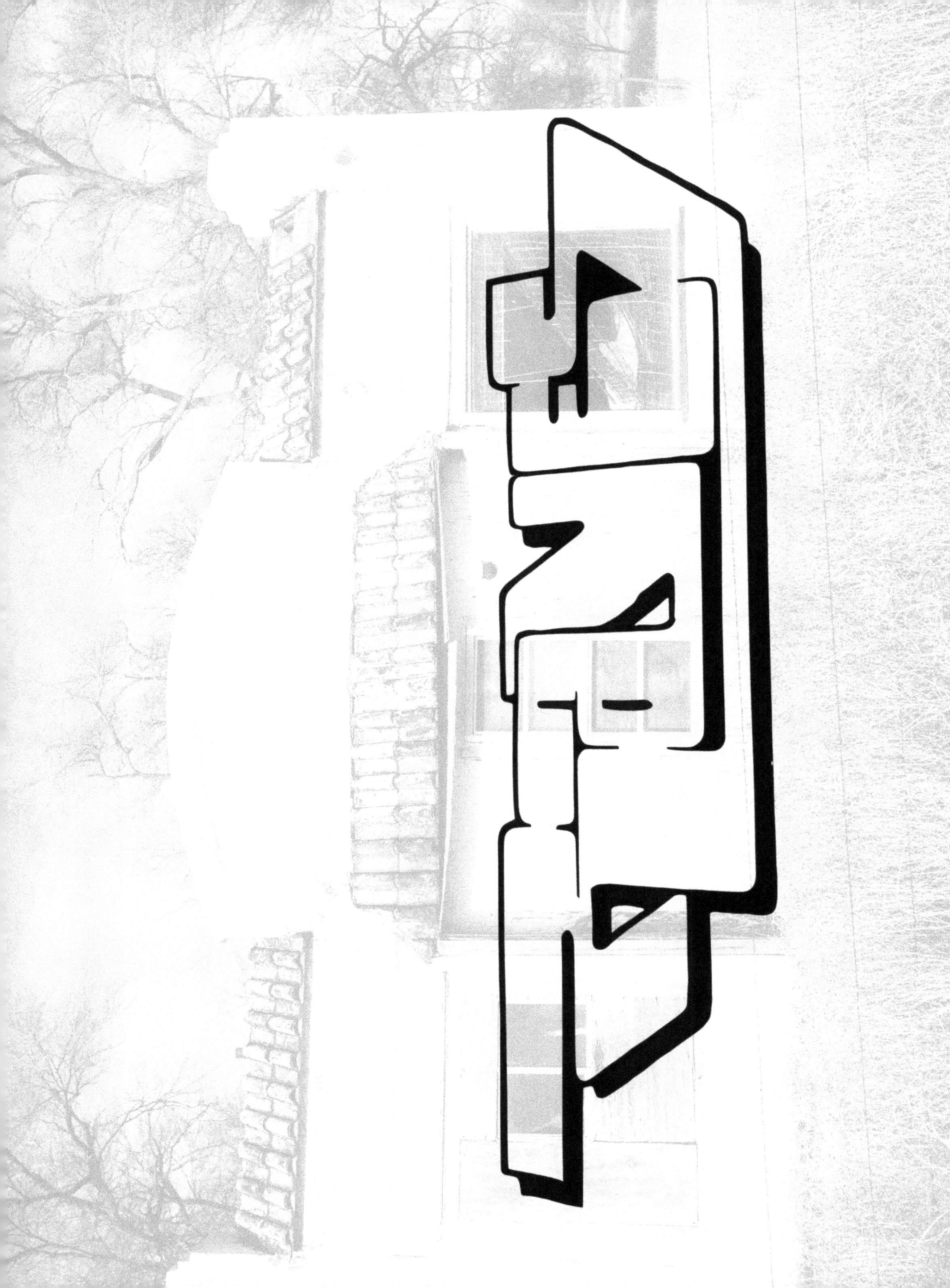

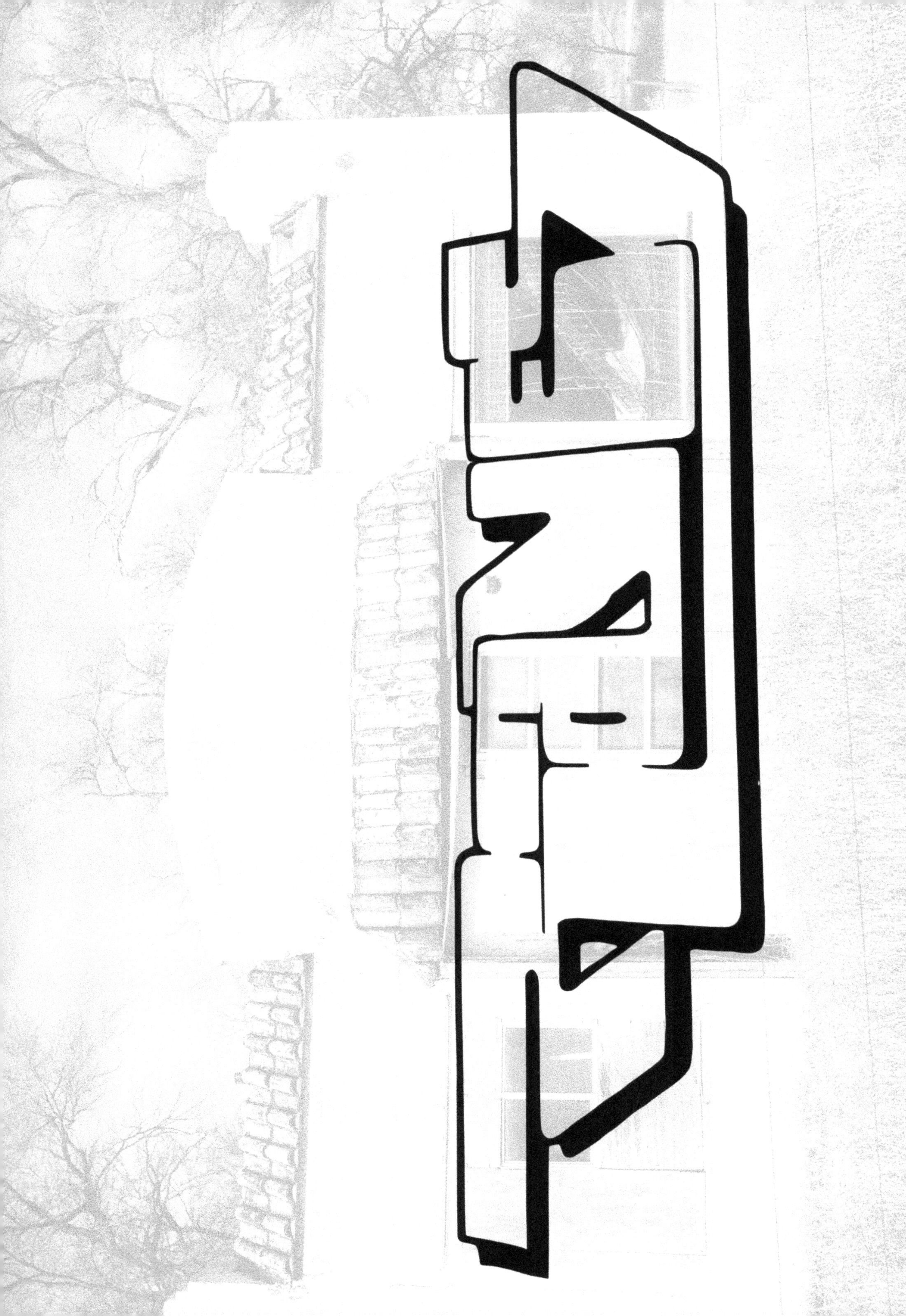

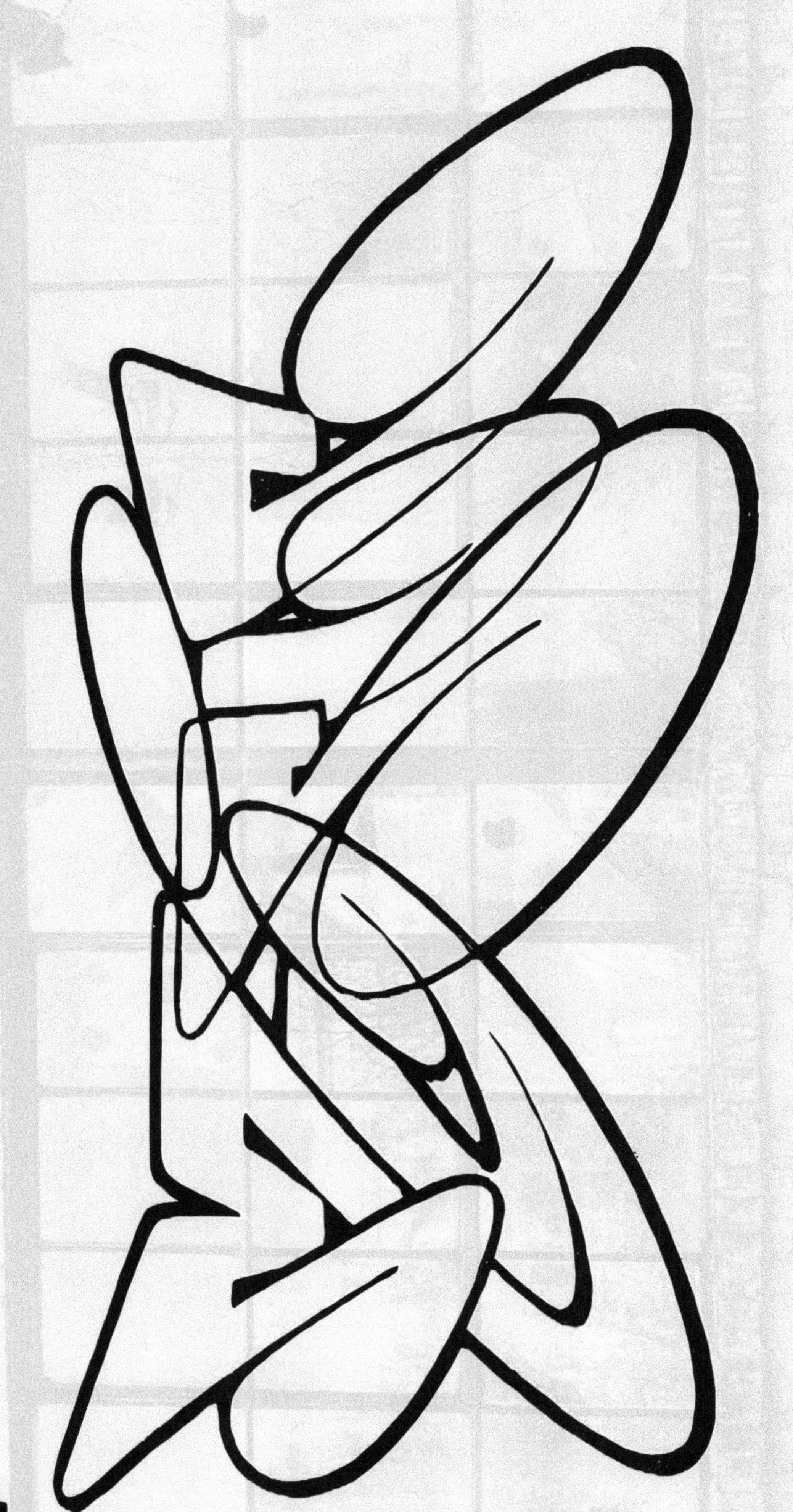

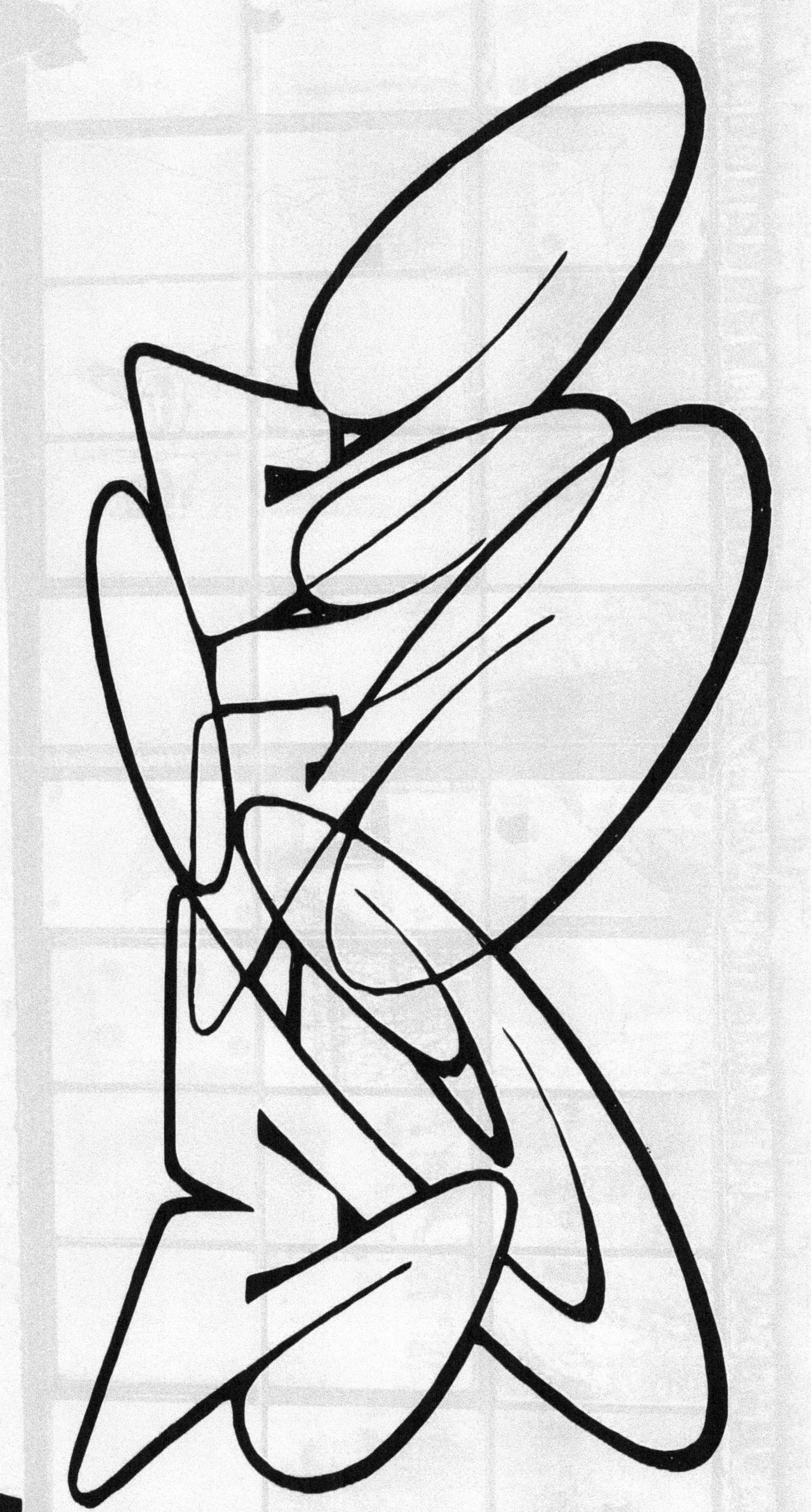

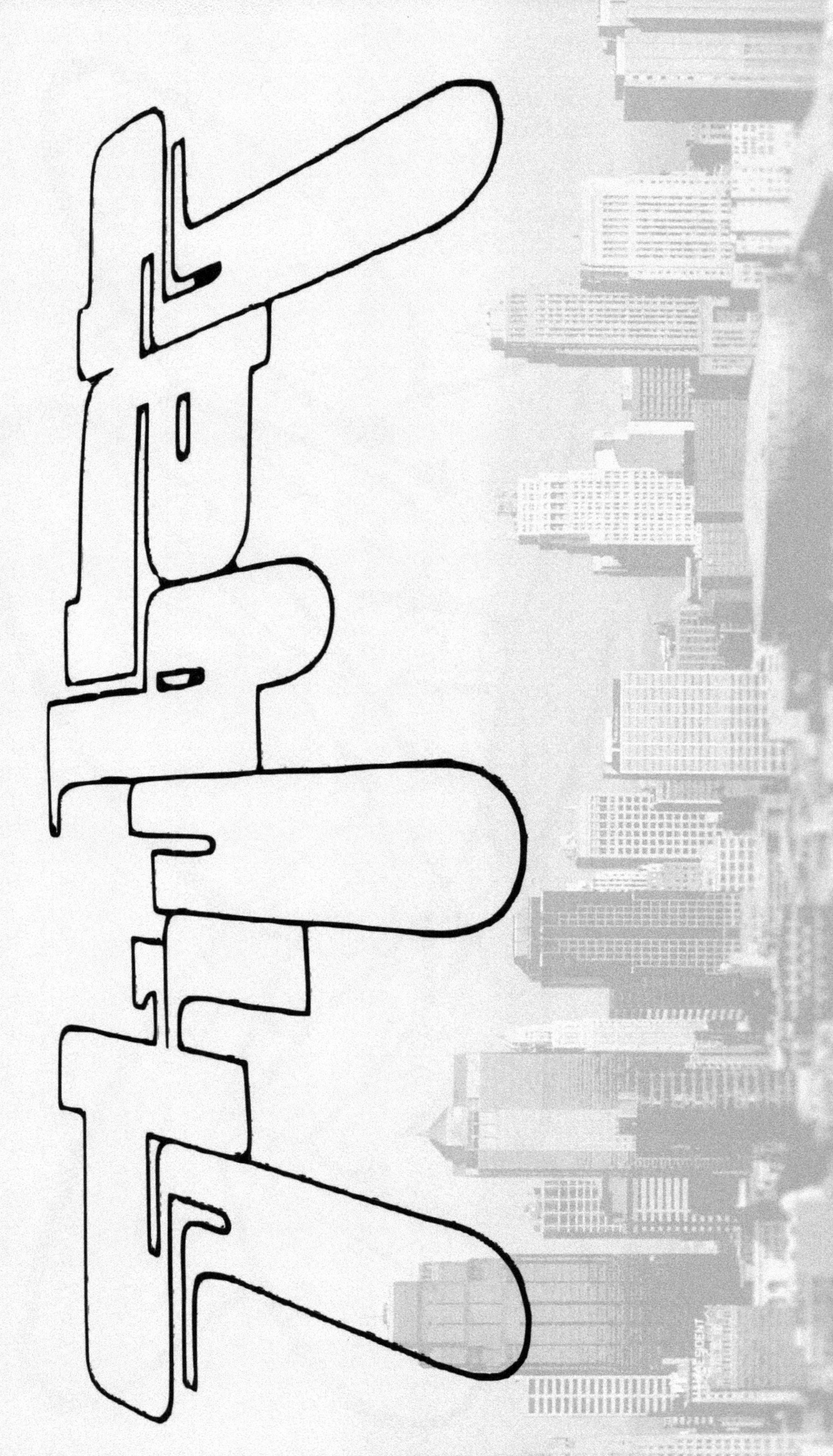

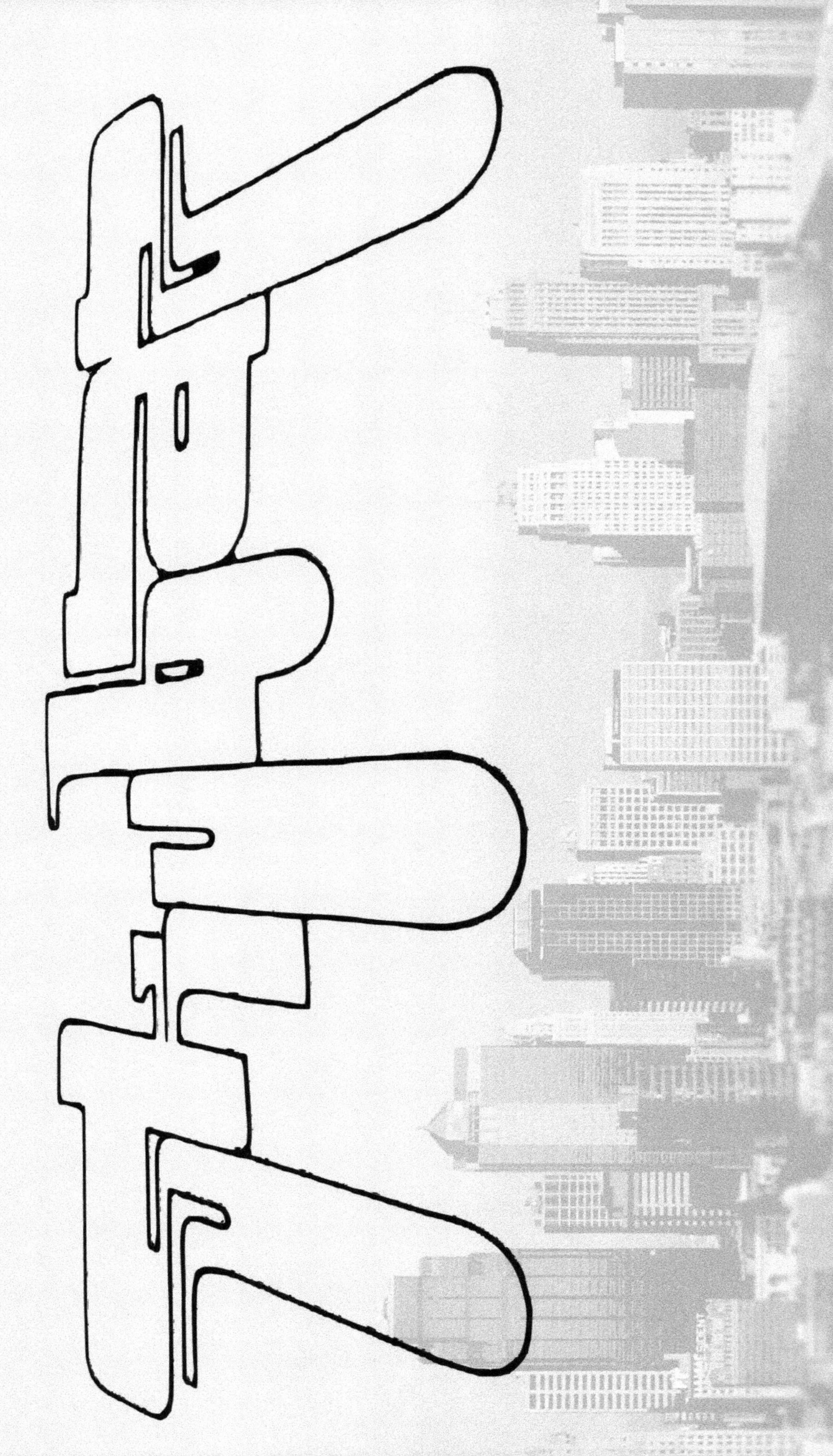

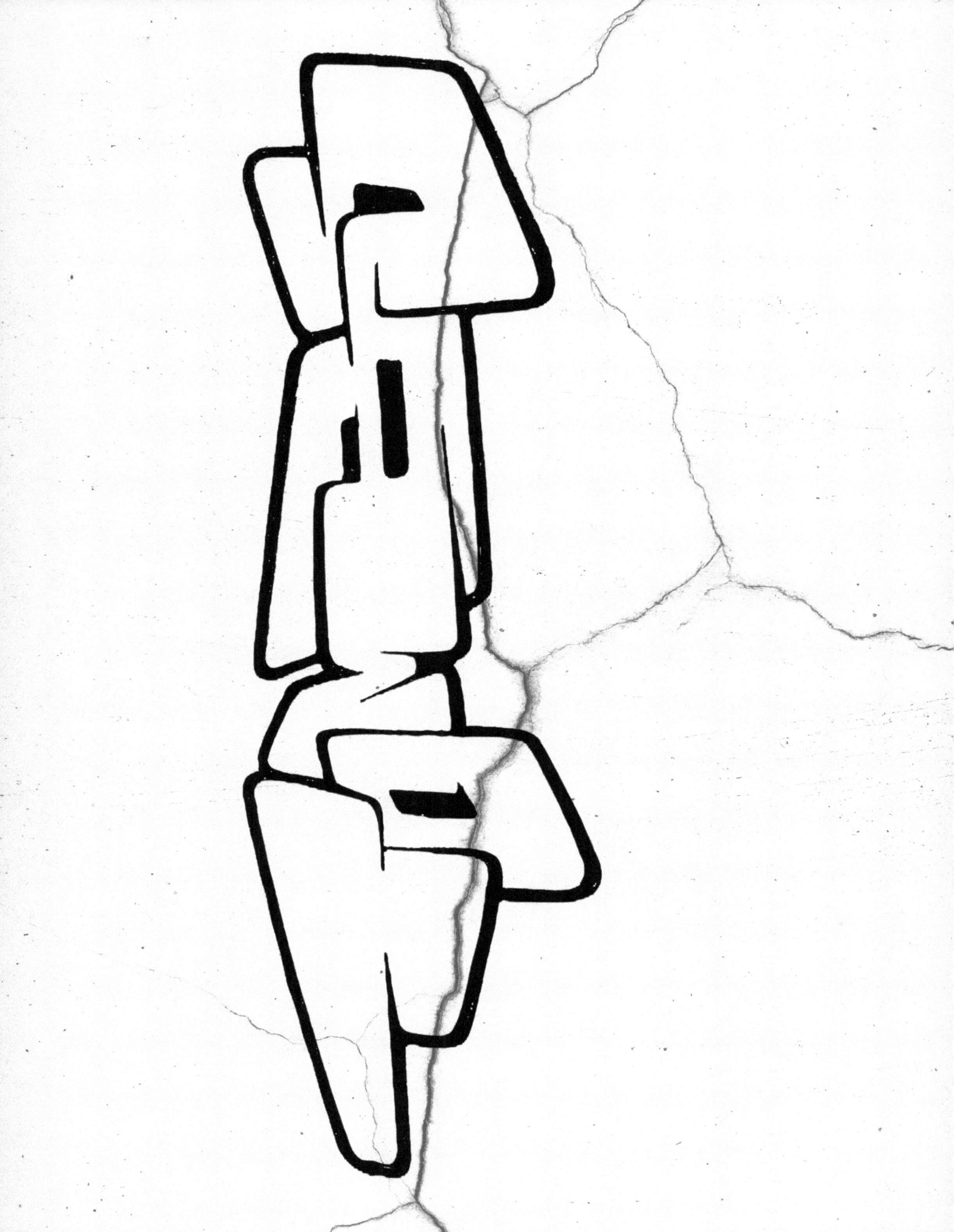

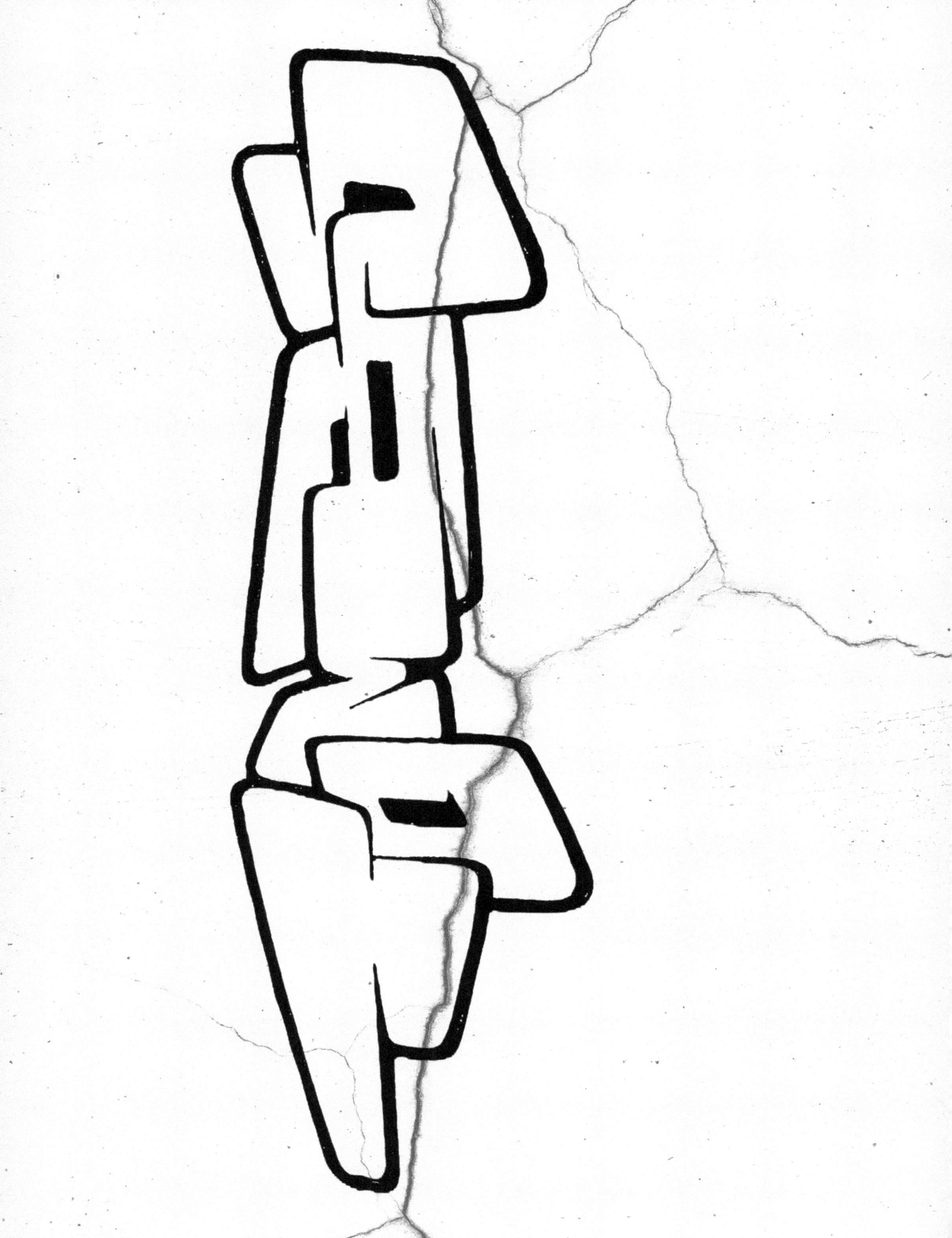

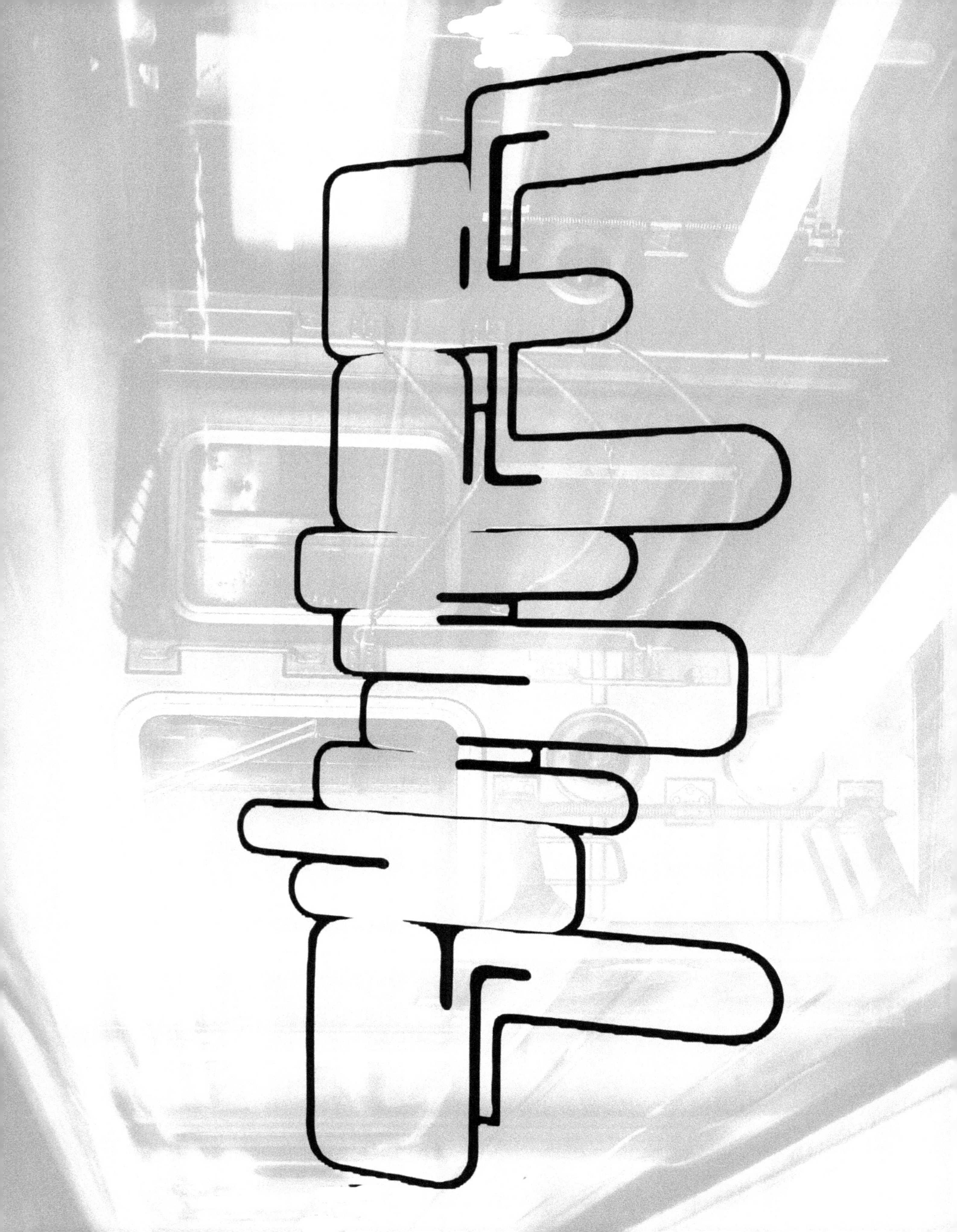

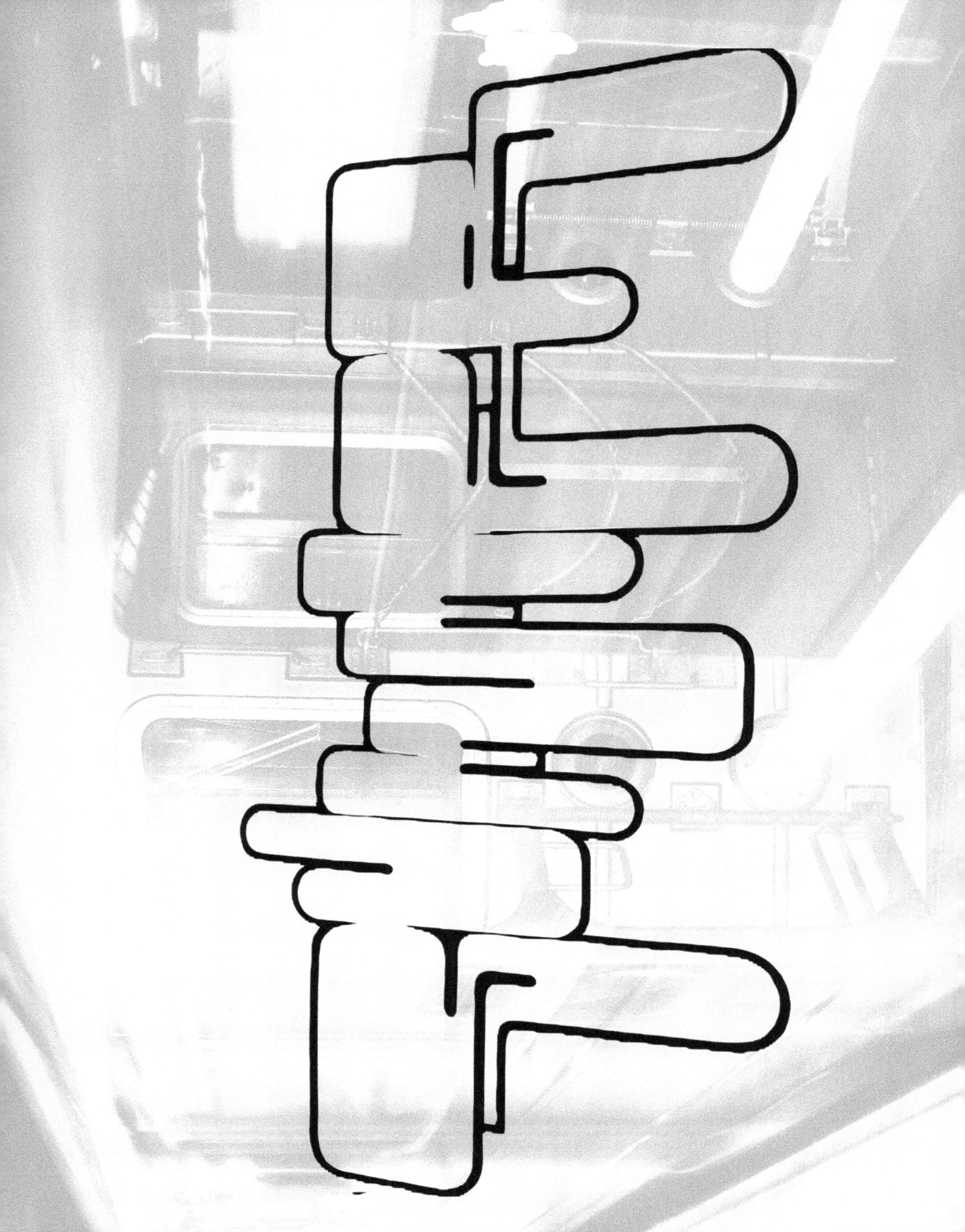

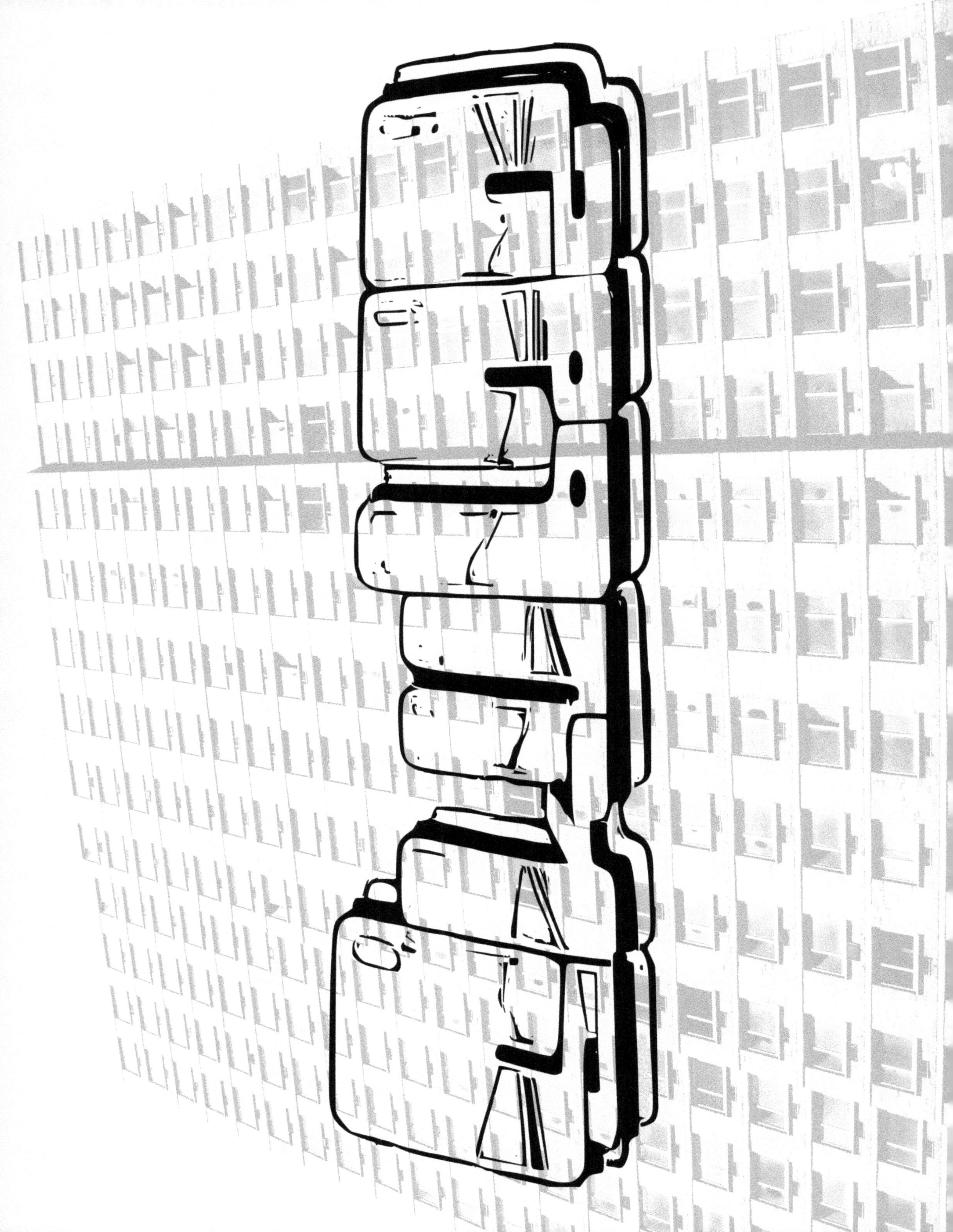

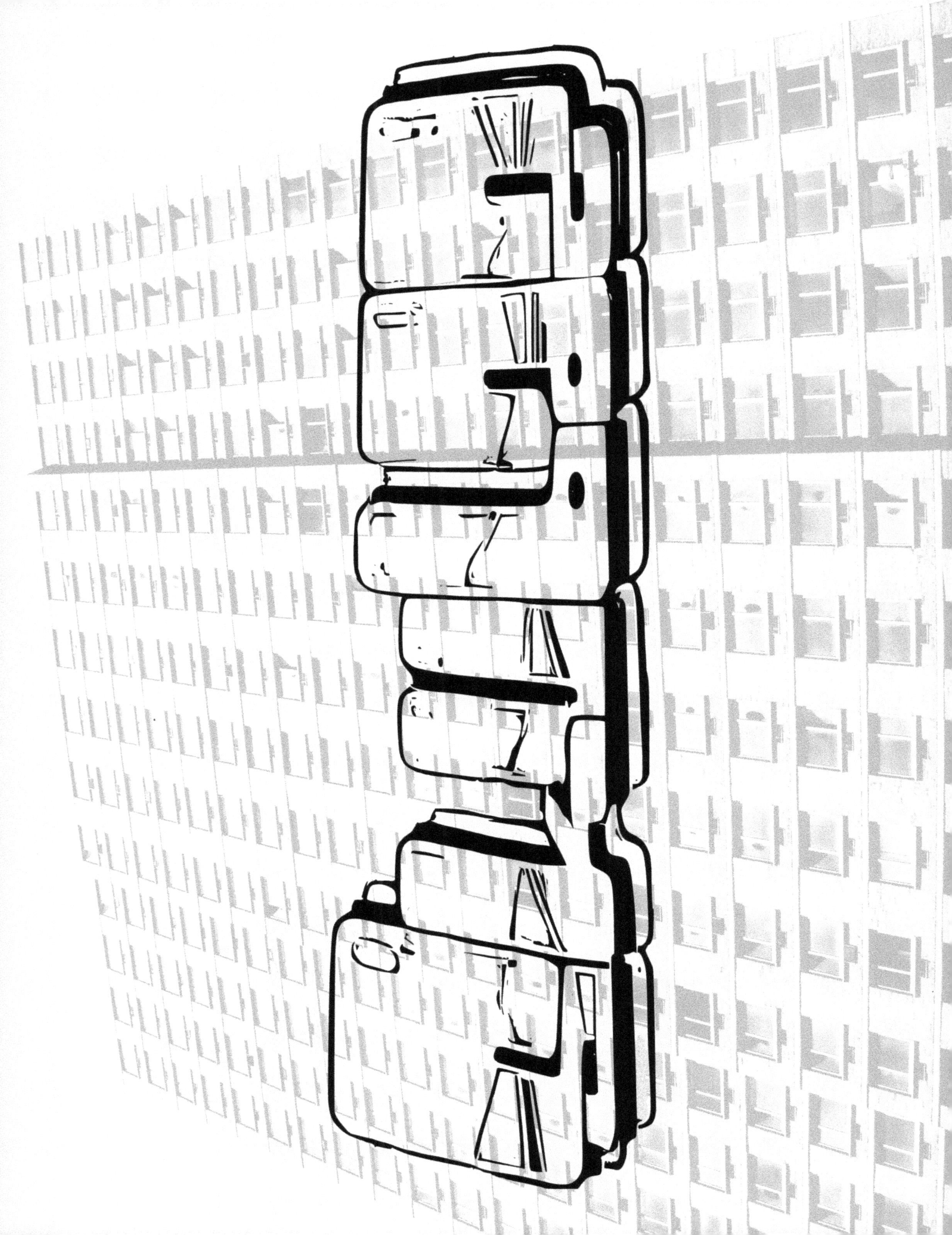

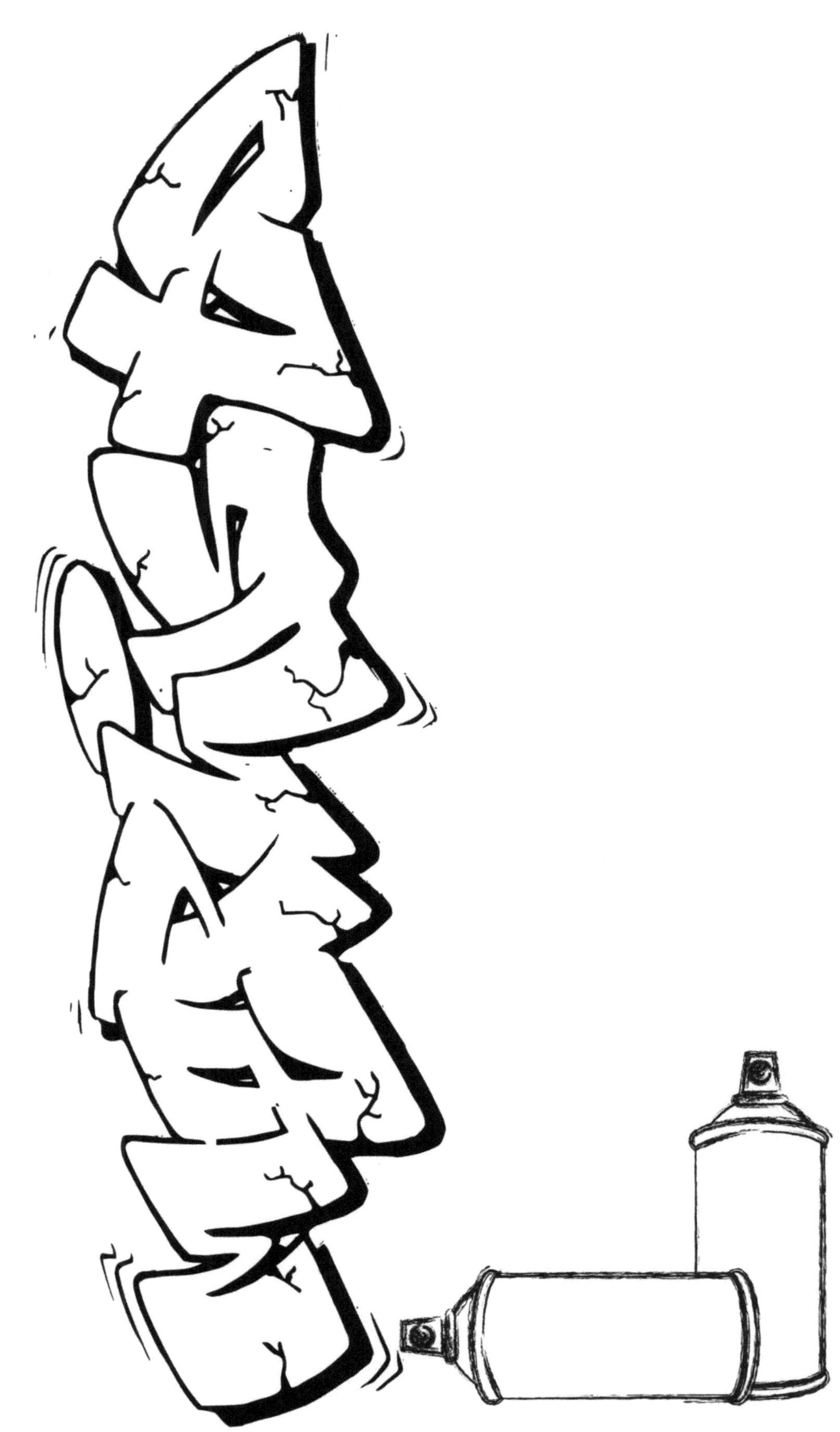

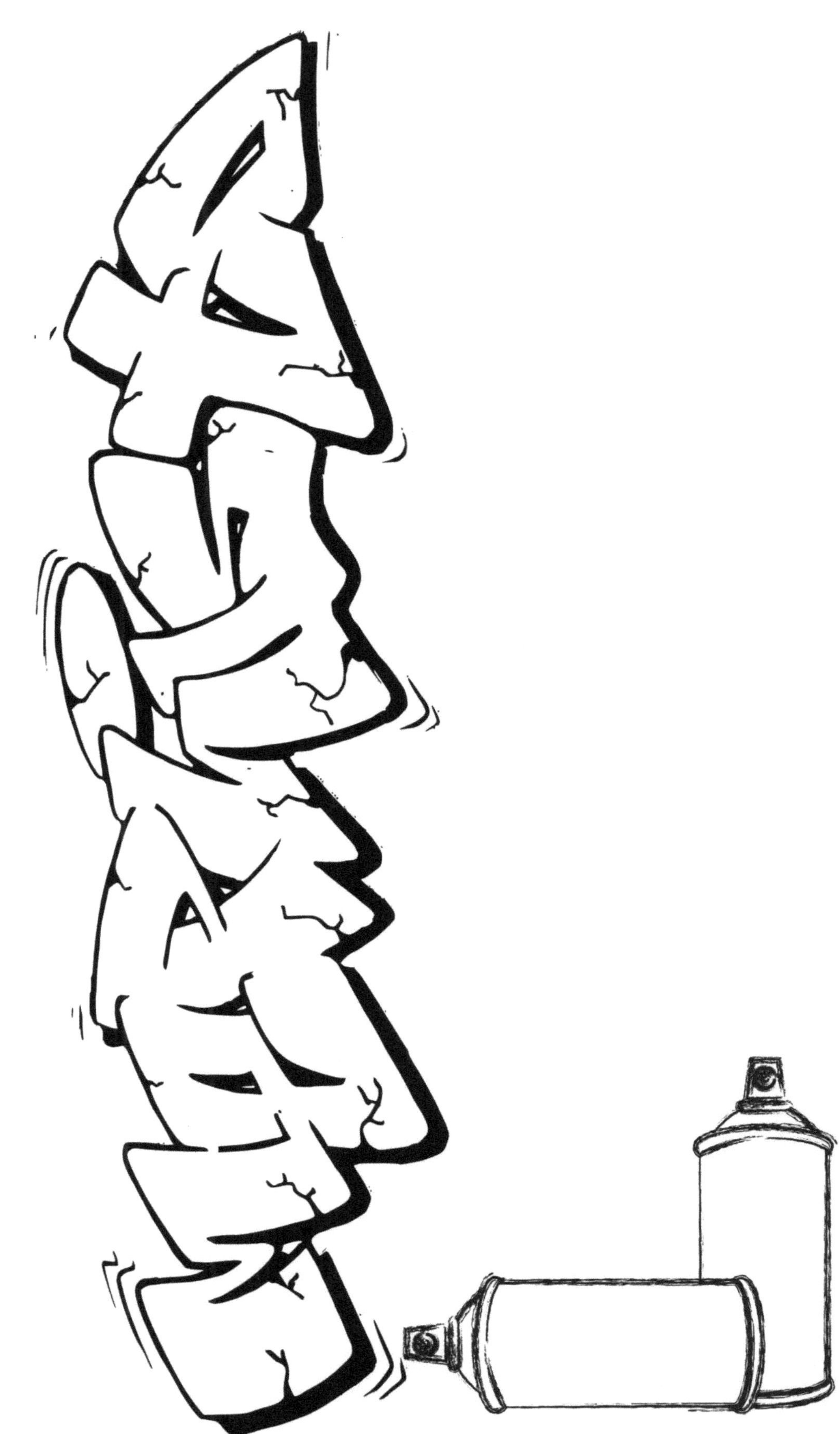

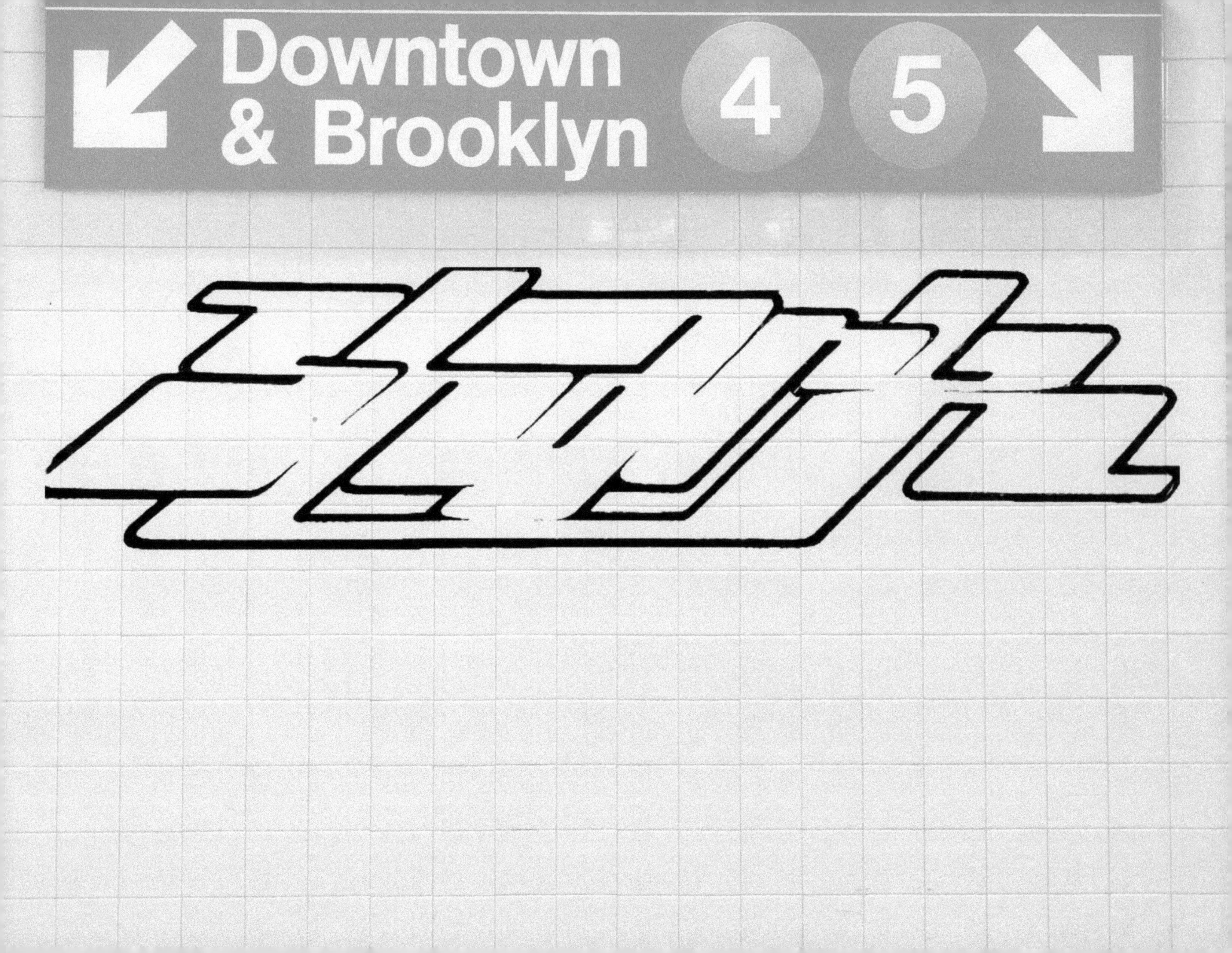

5
4
Downtown
& Brooklyn

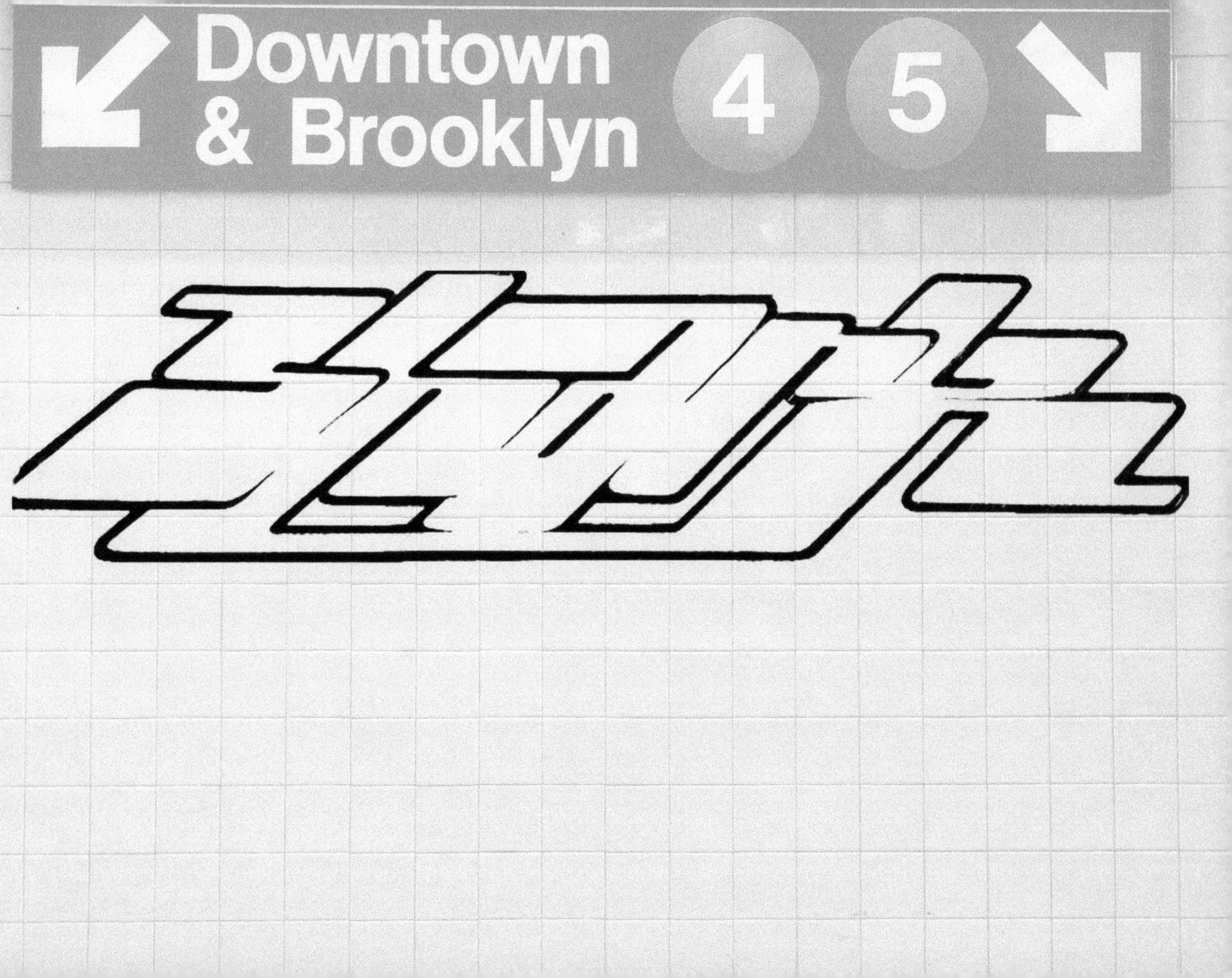

Downtown
& Brooklyn
4
5

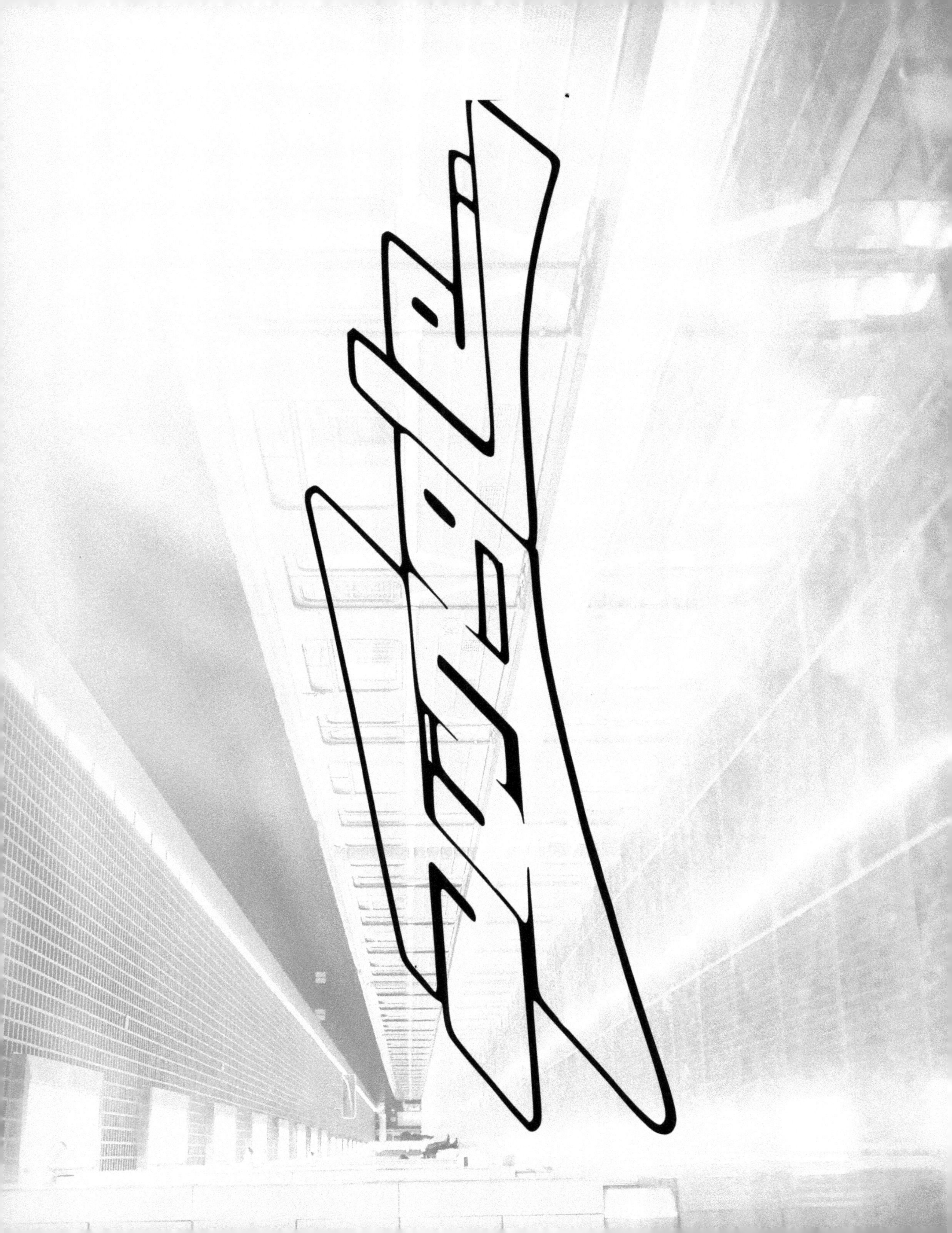

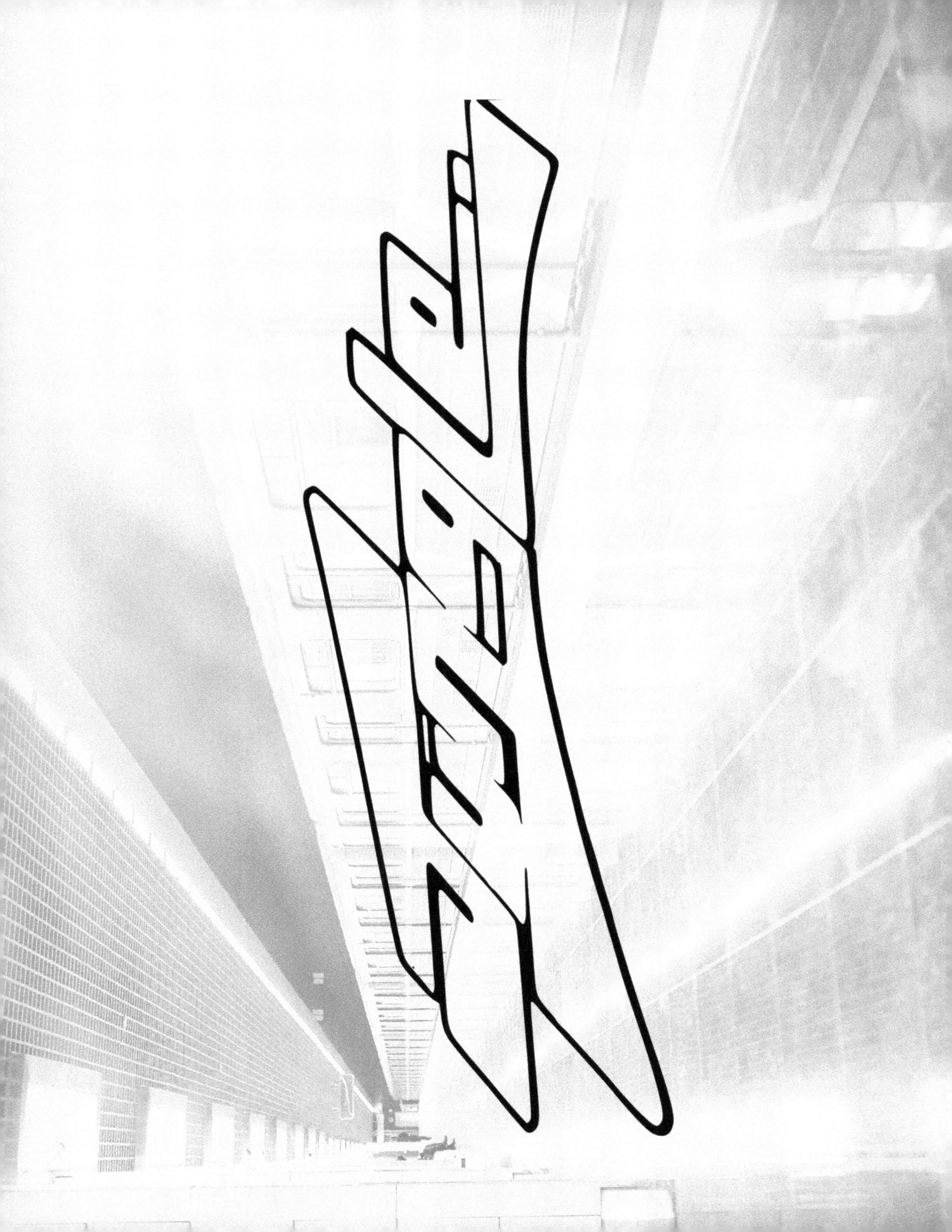

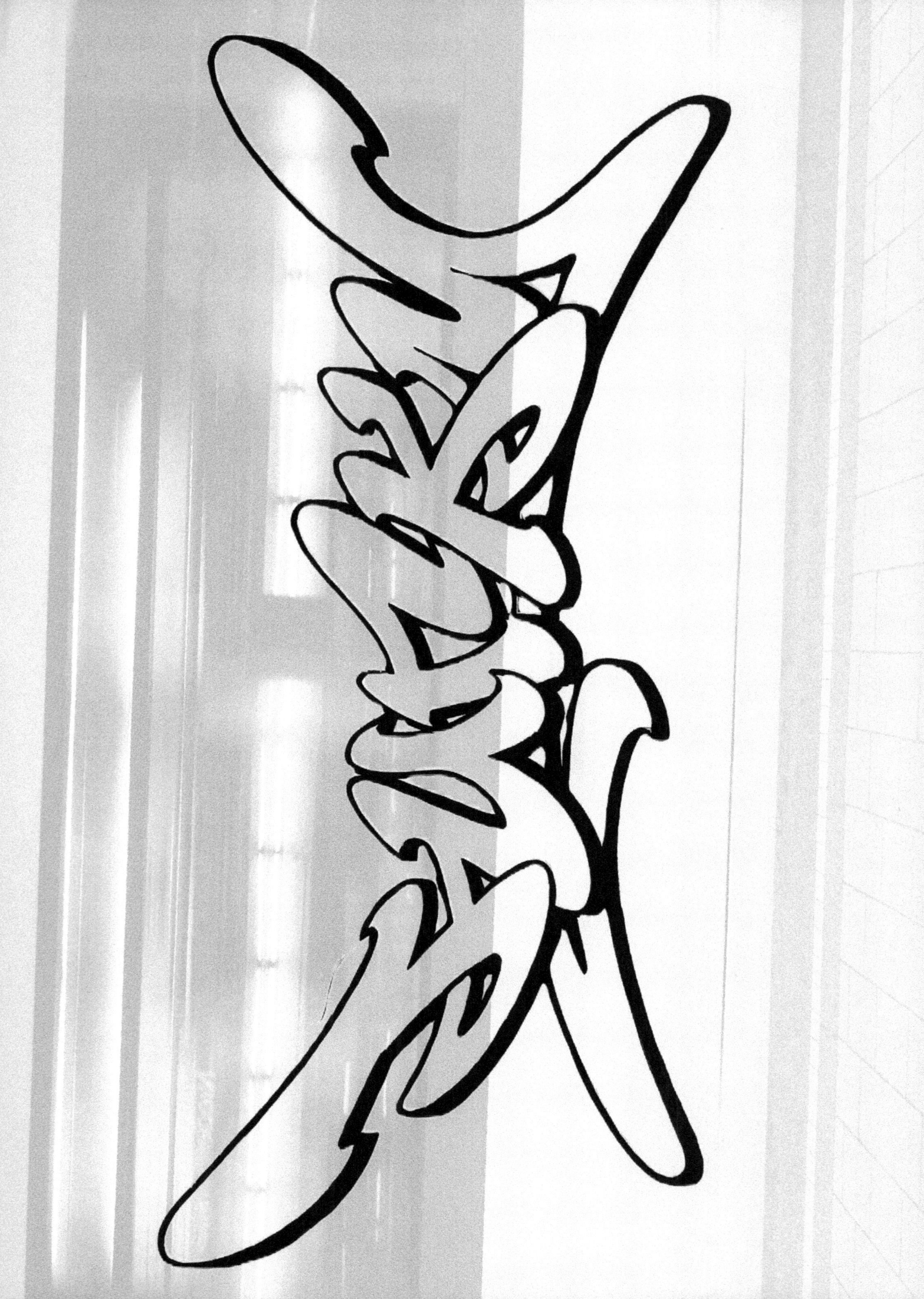

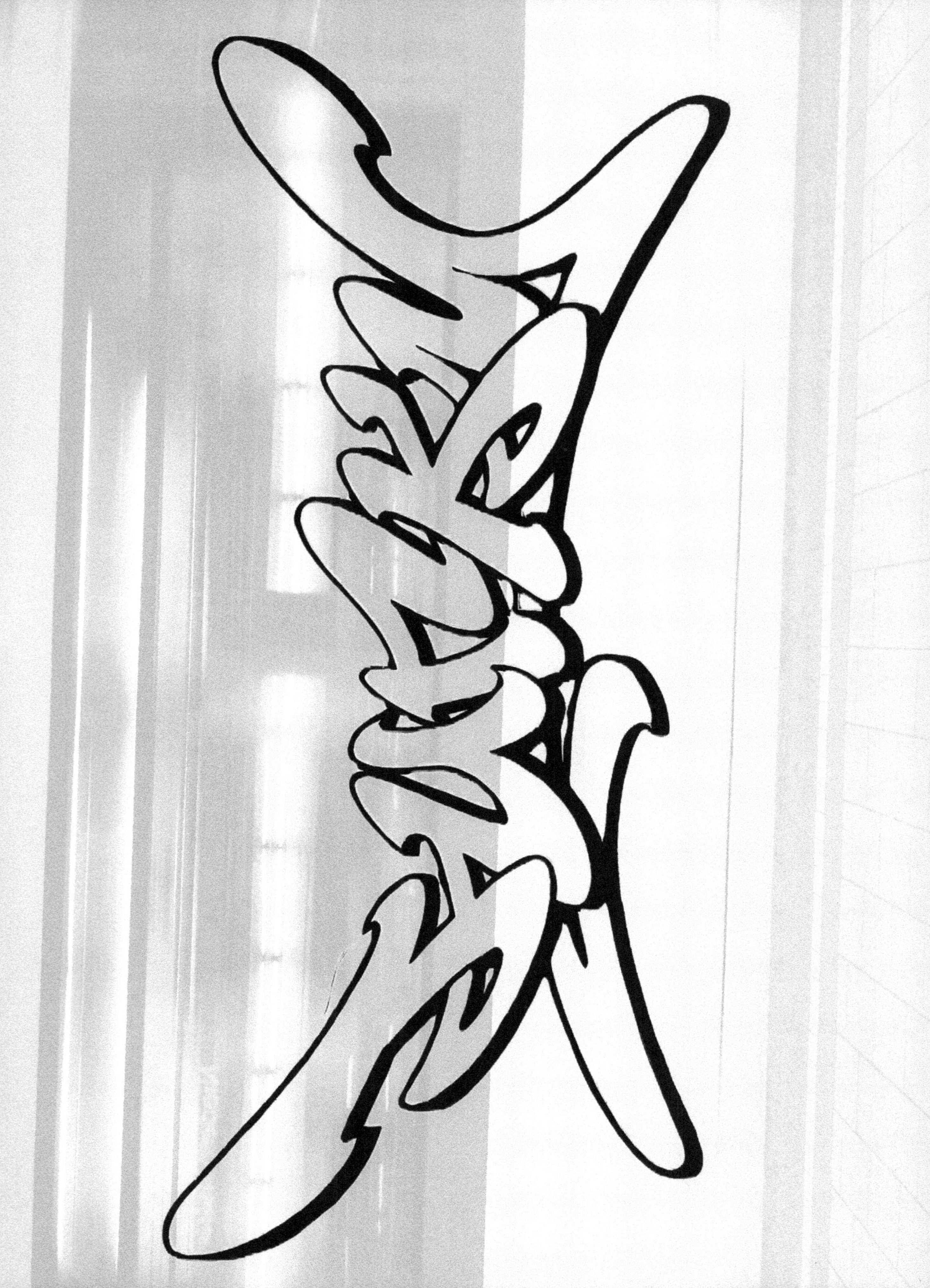

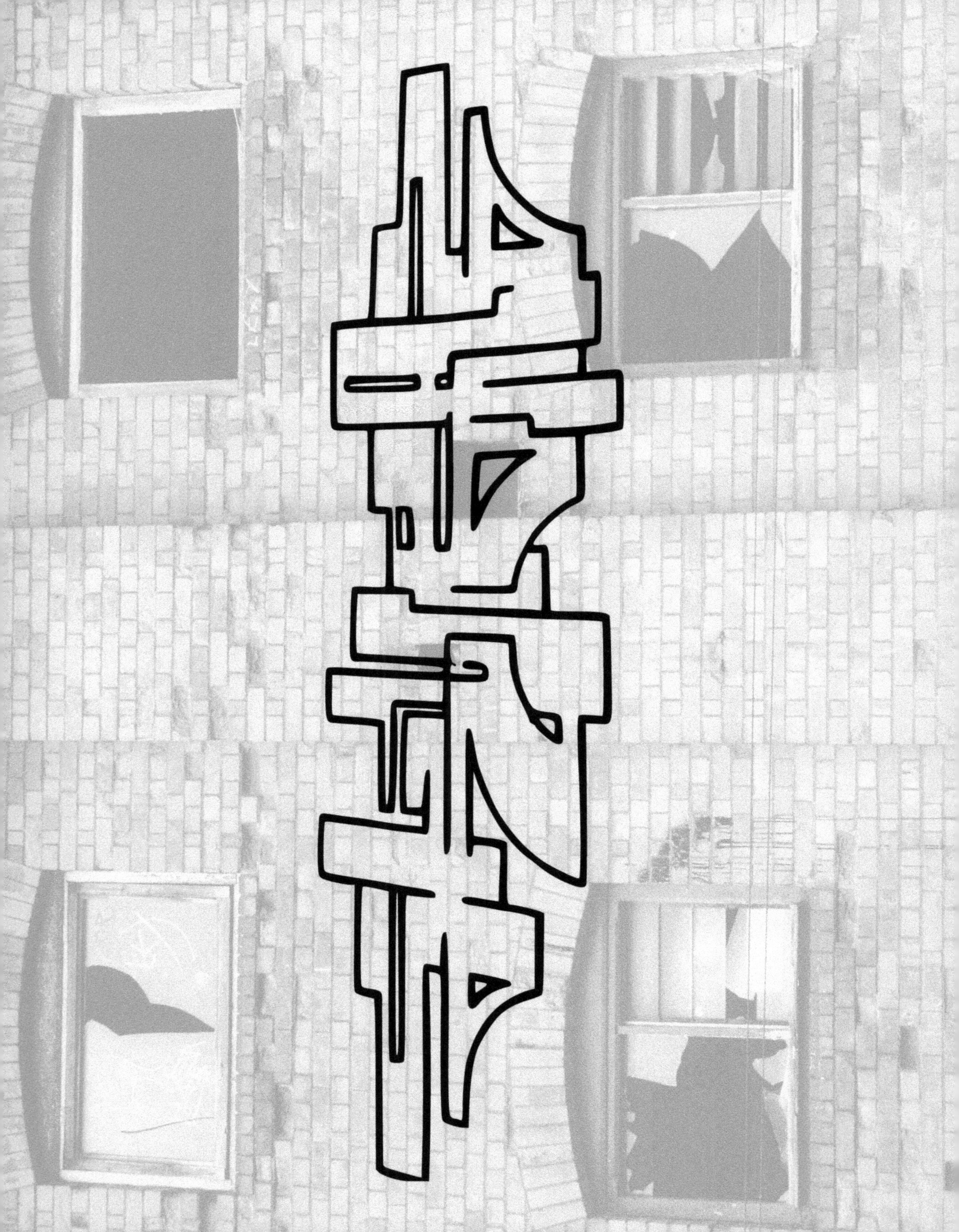

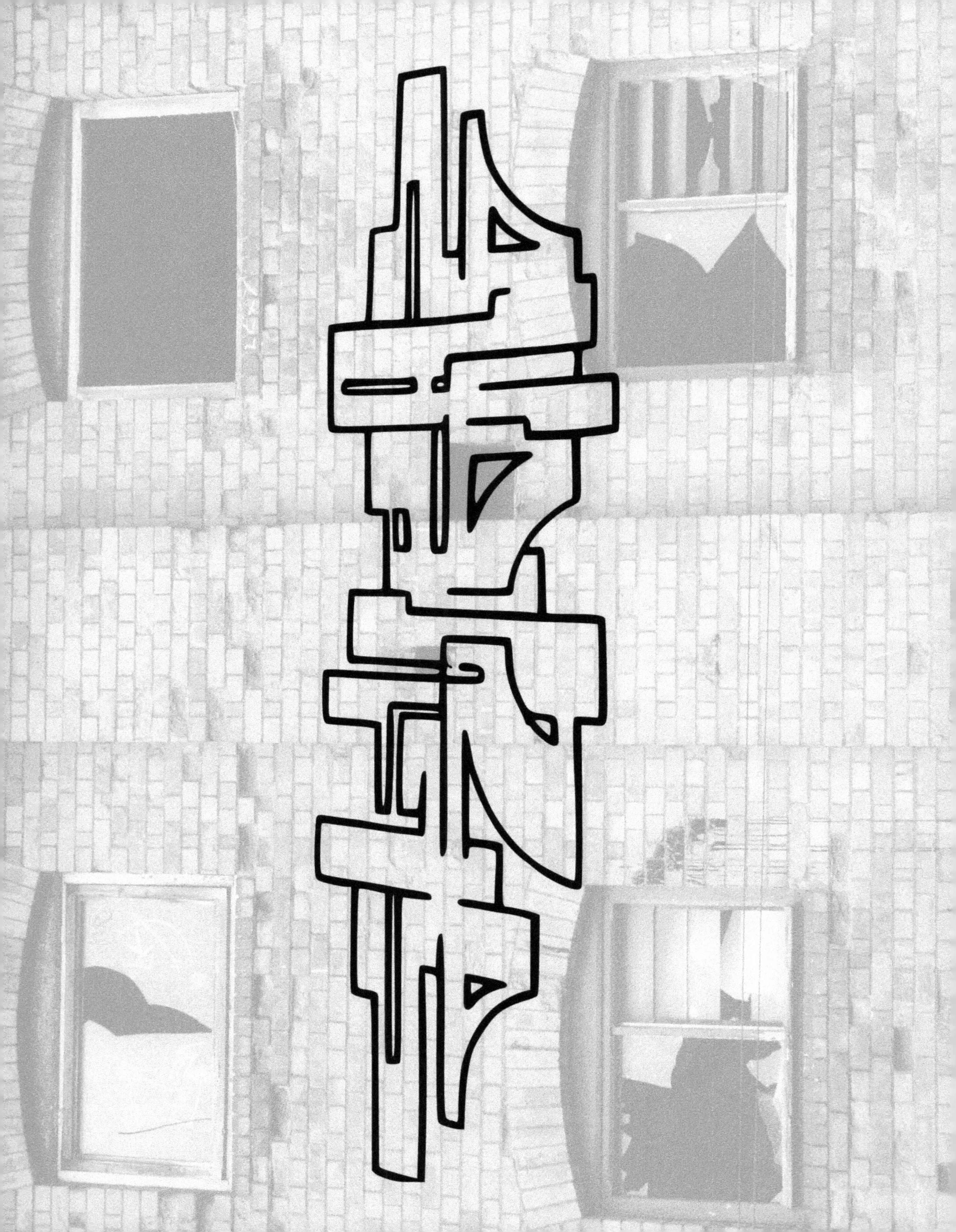

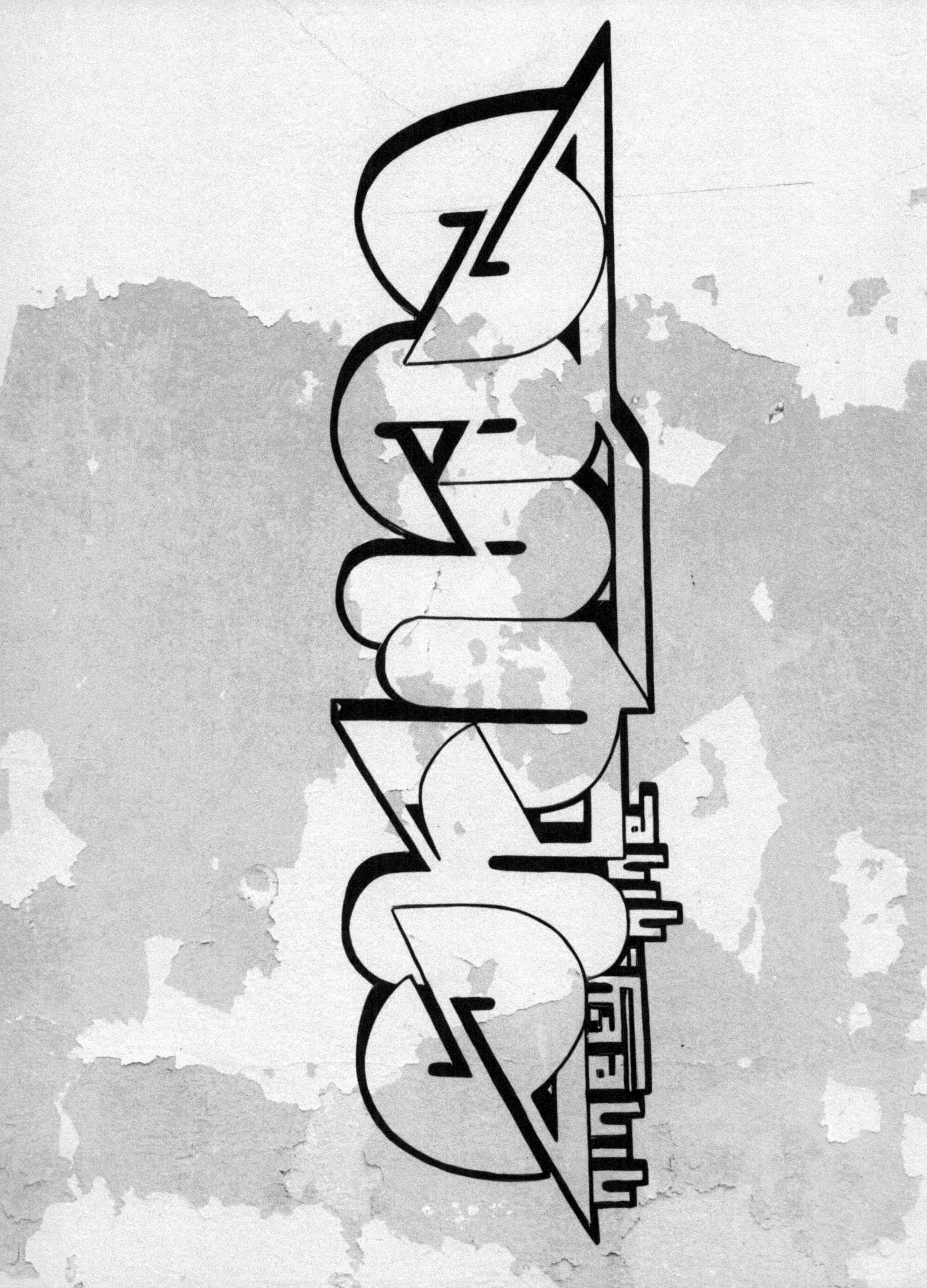

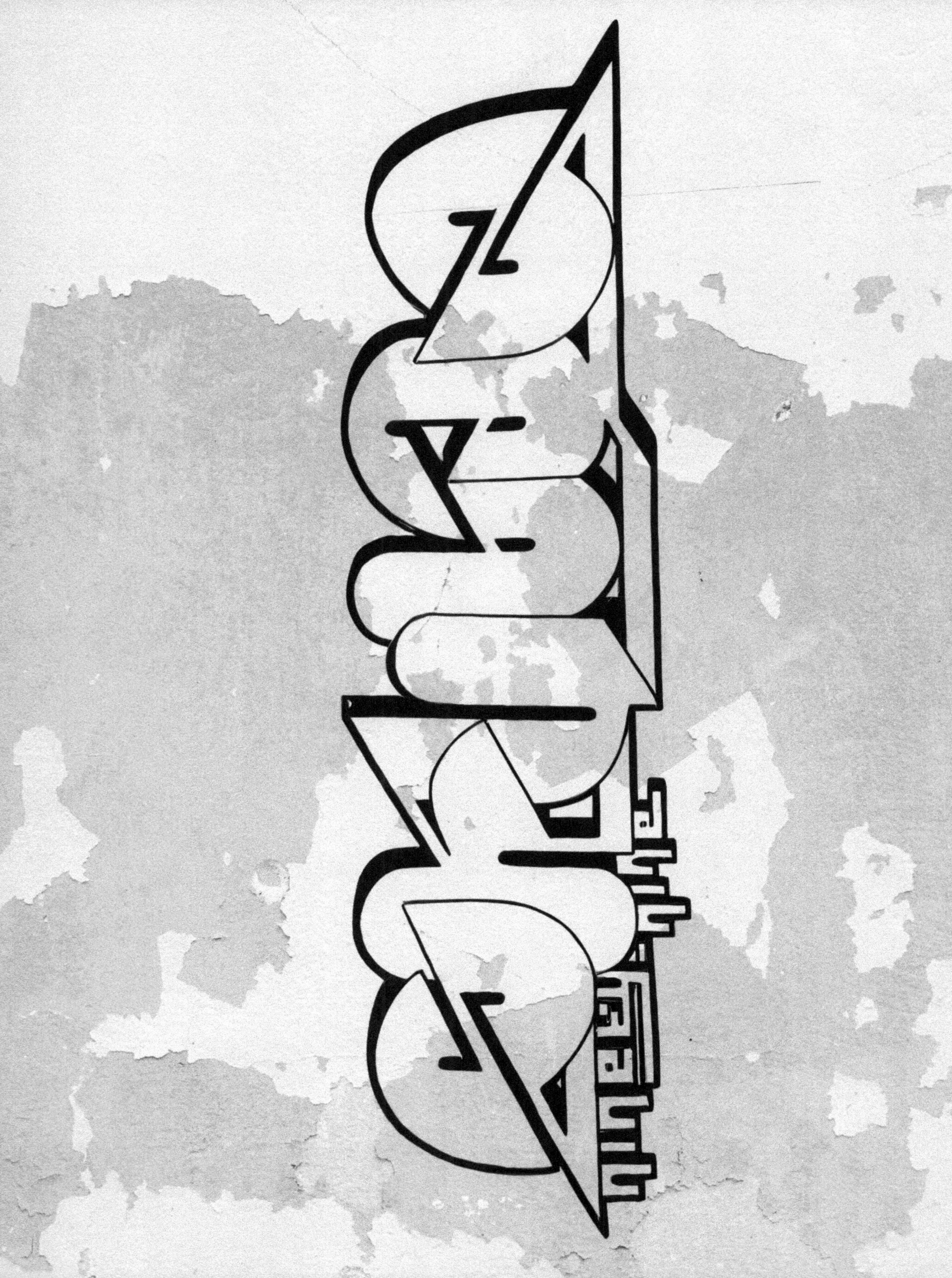

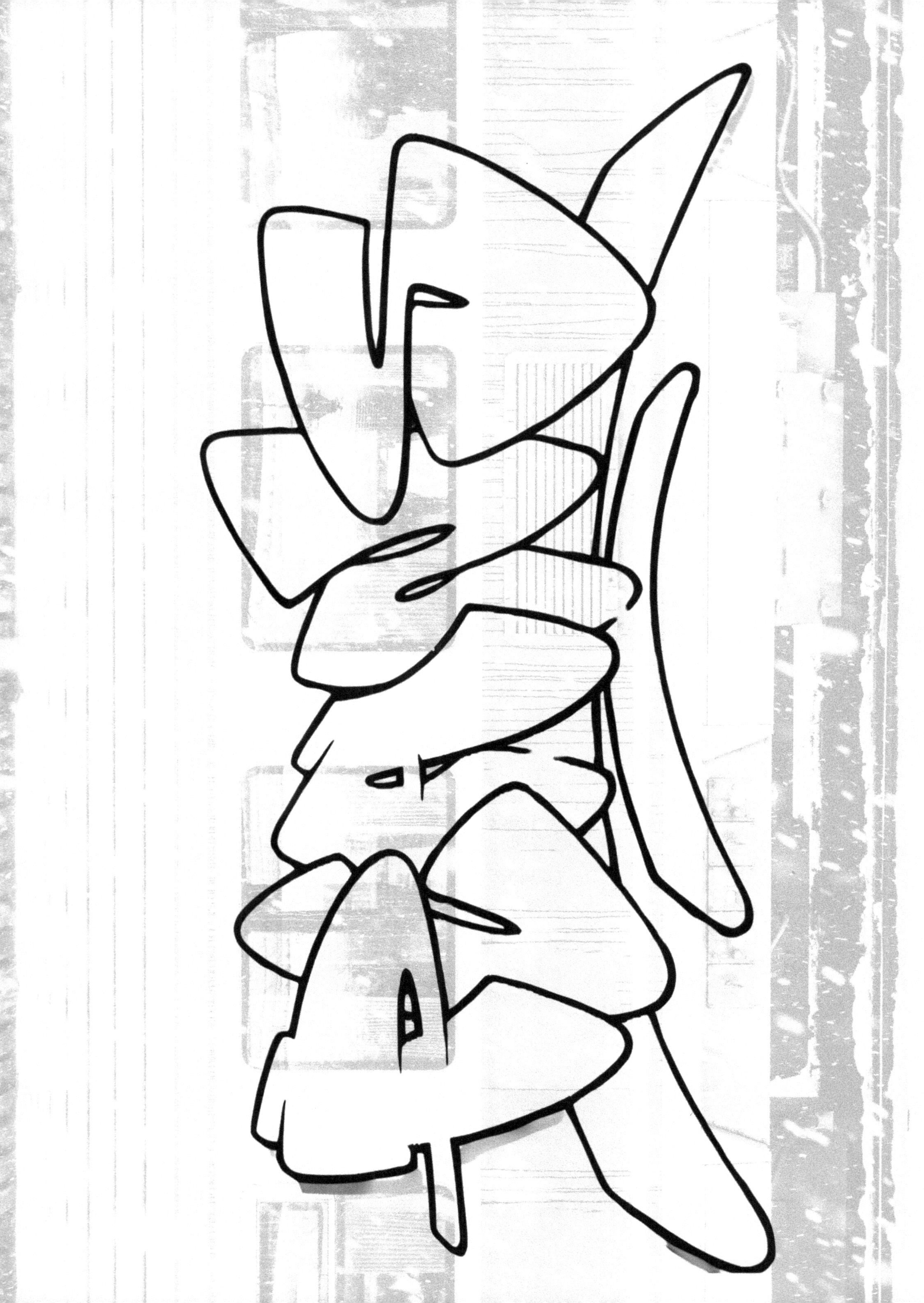

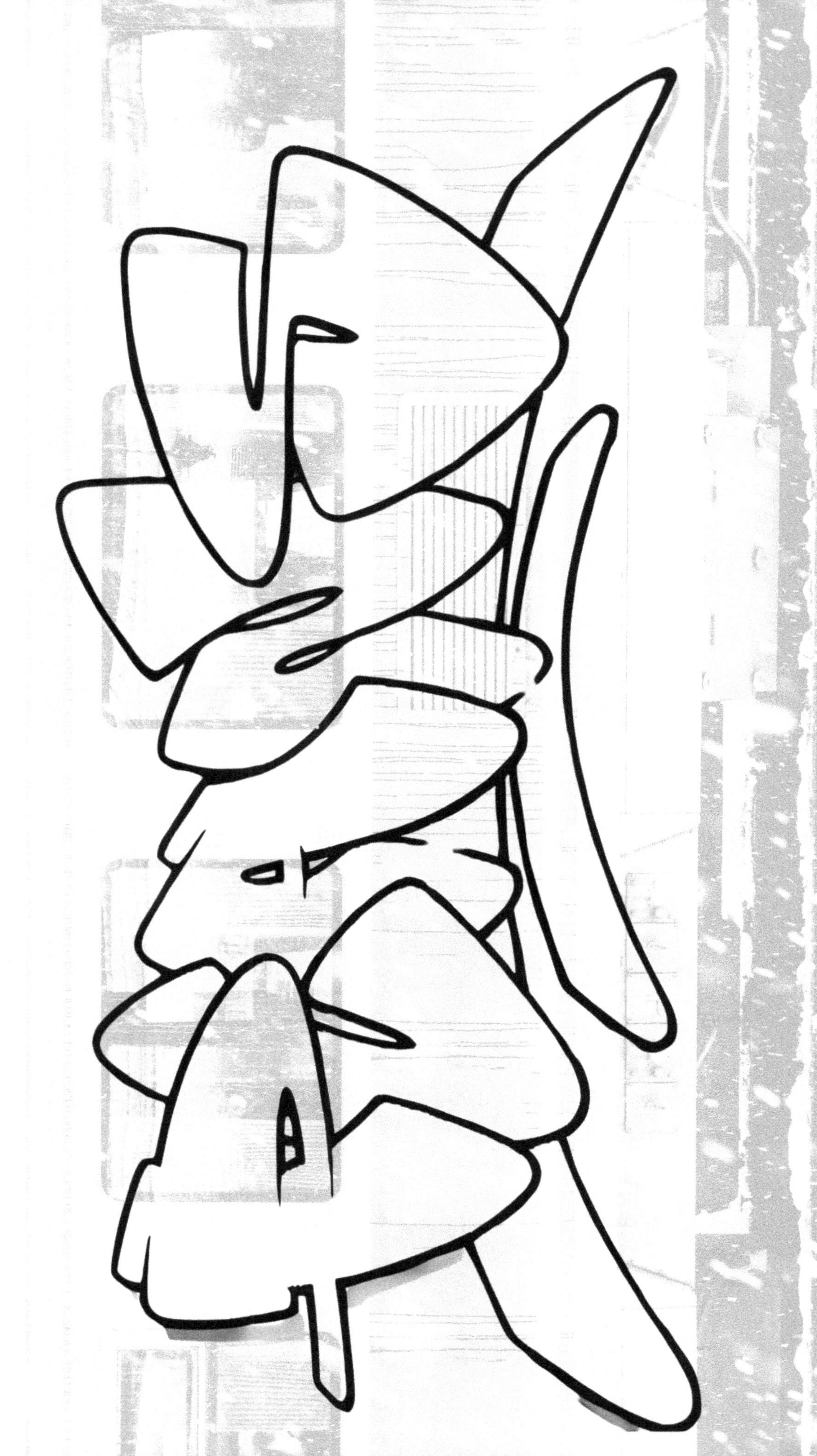

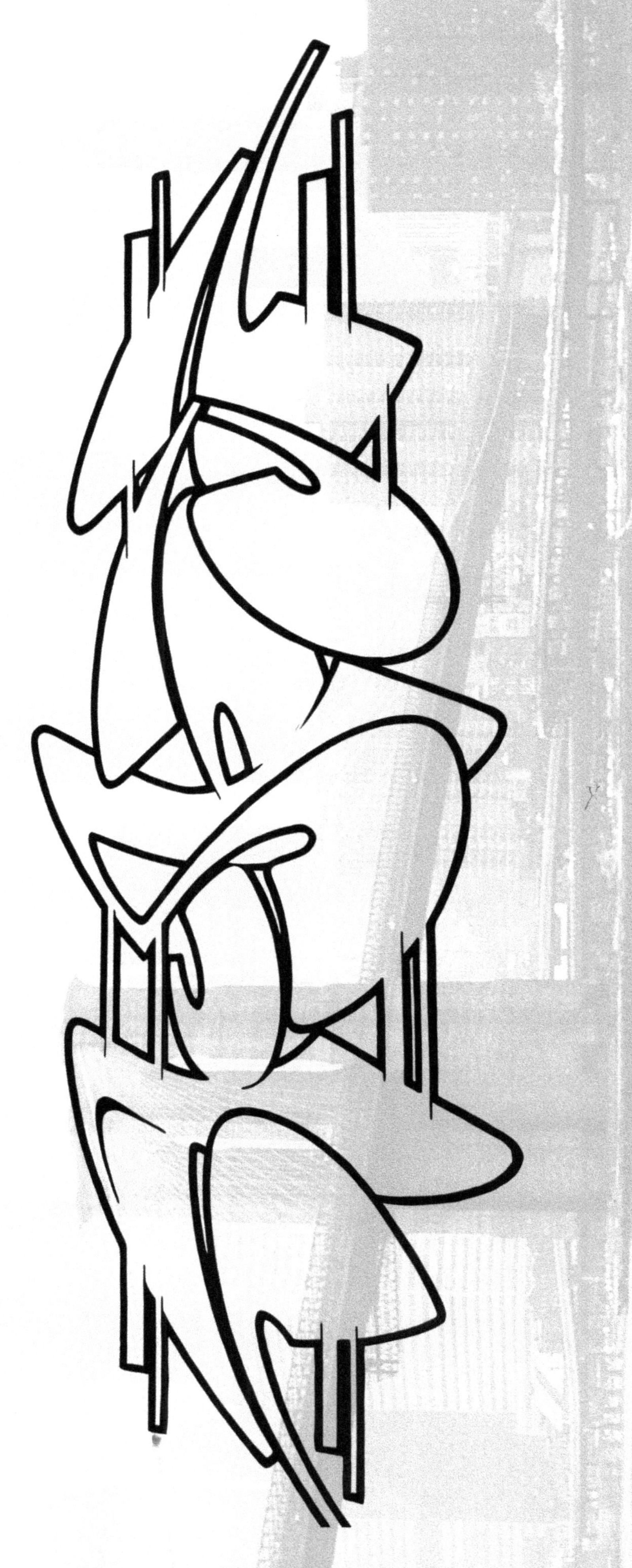

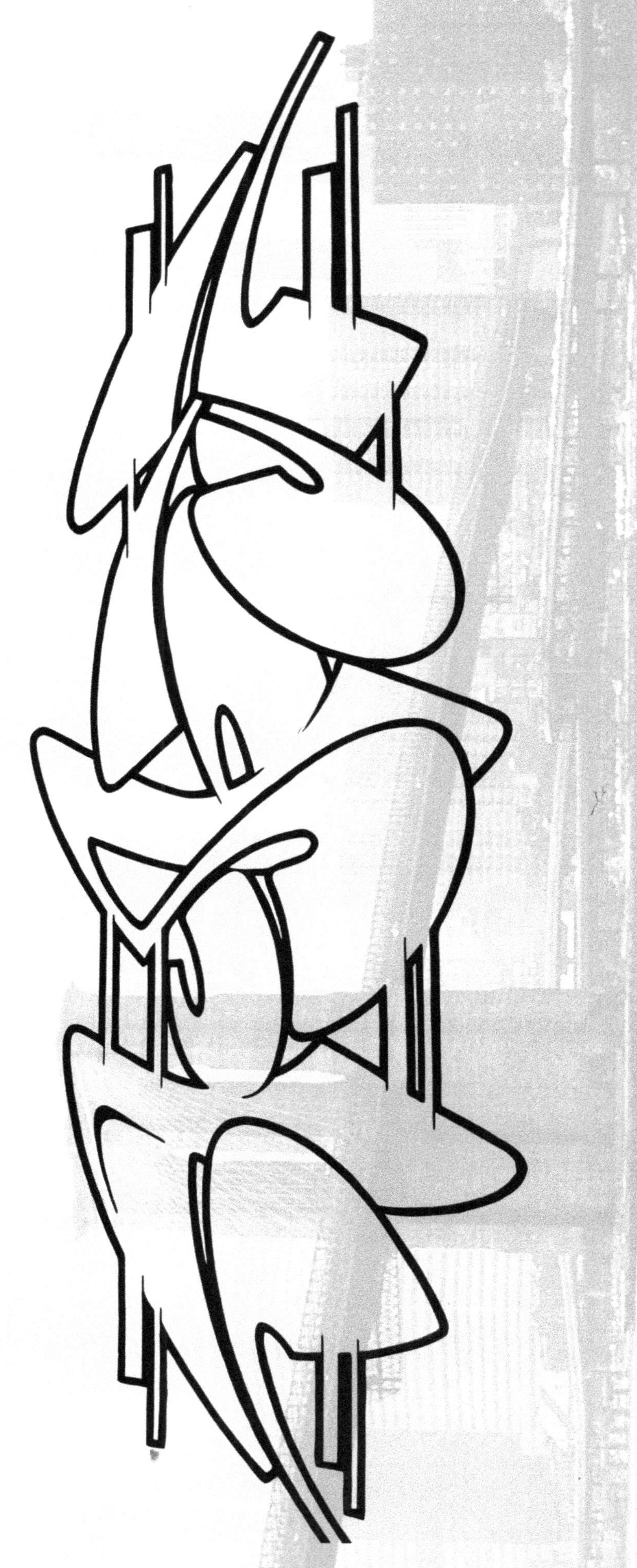

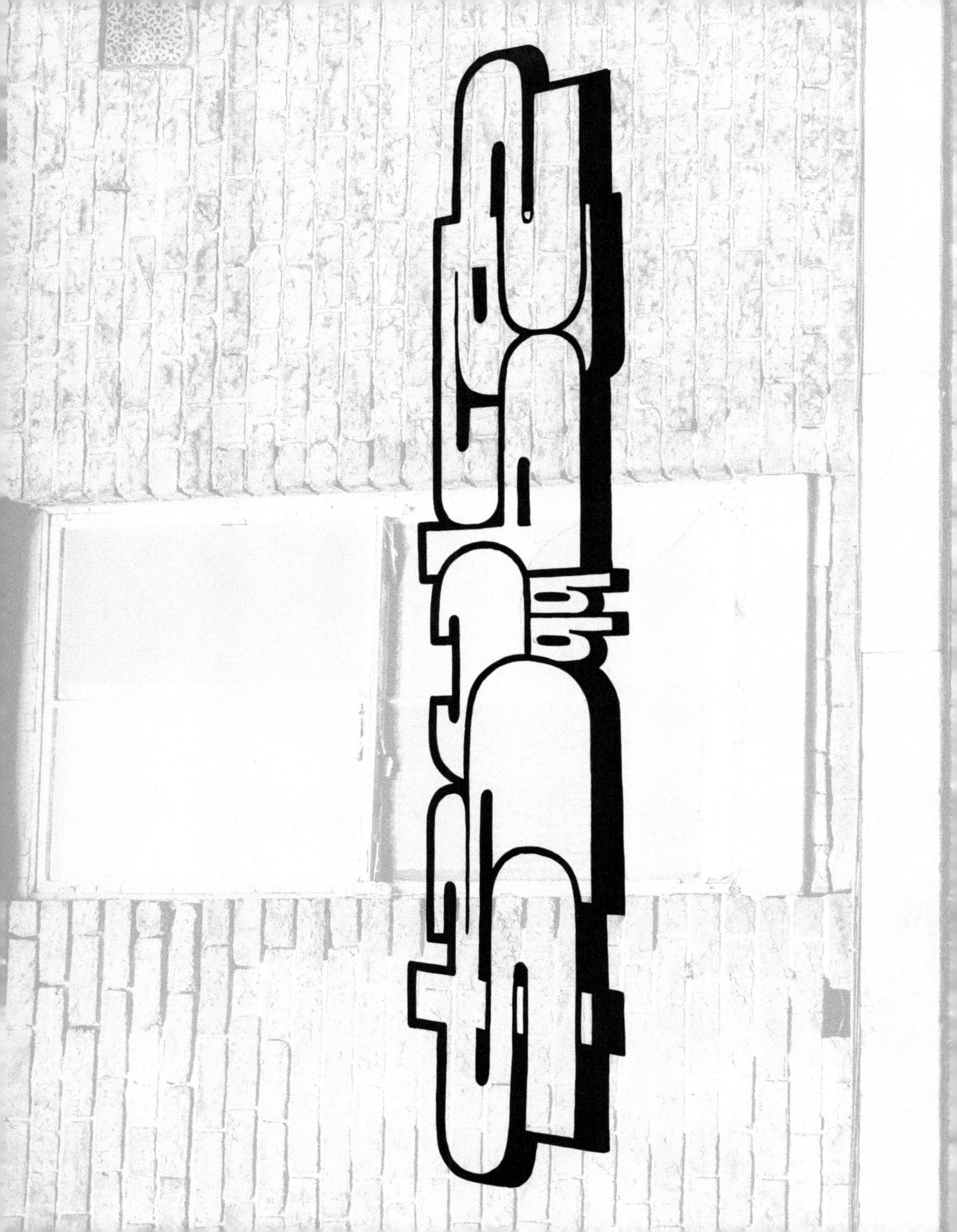

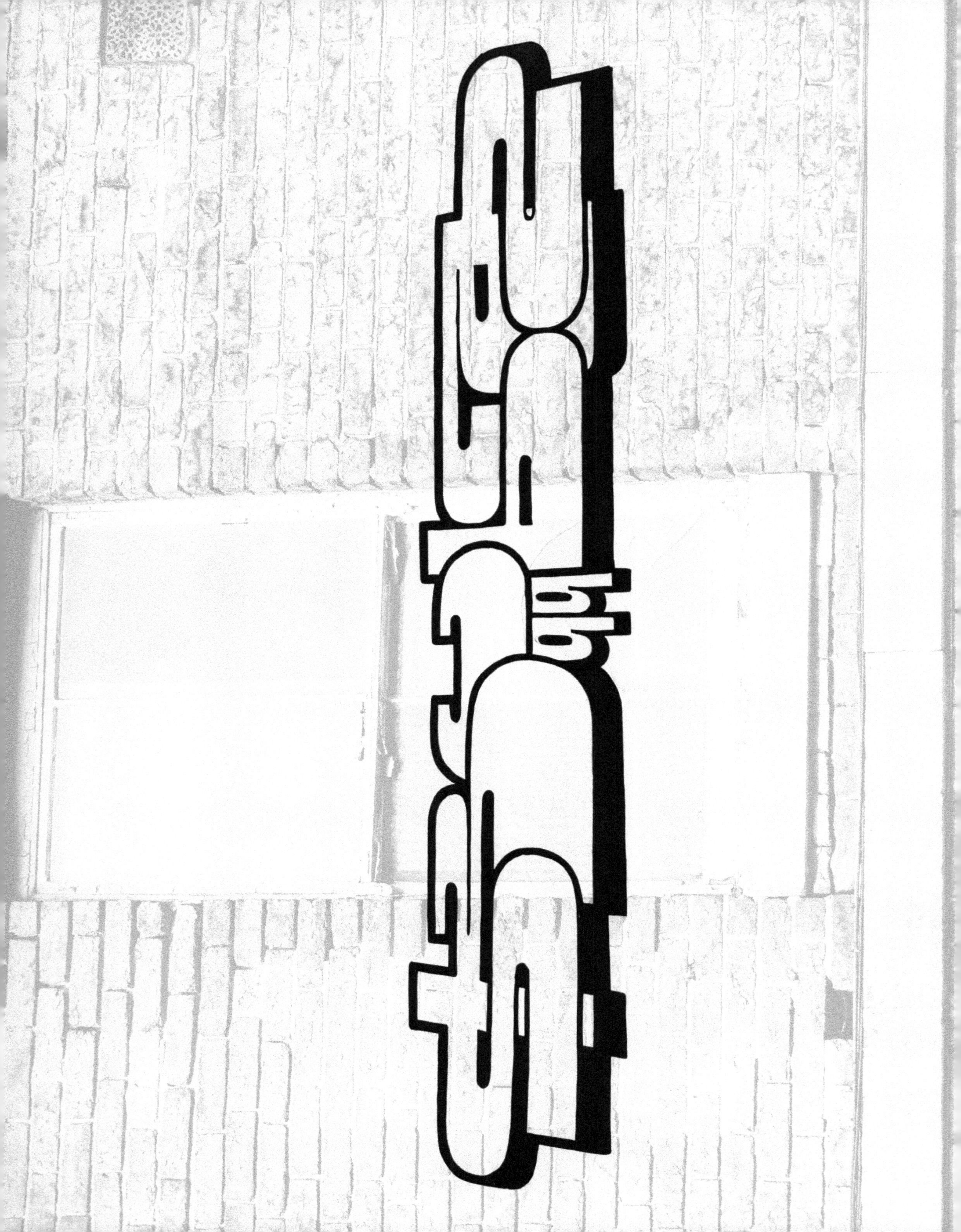

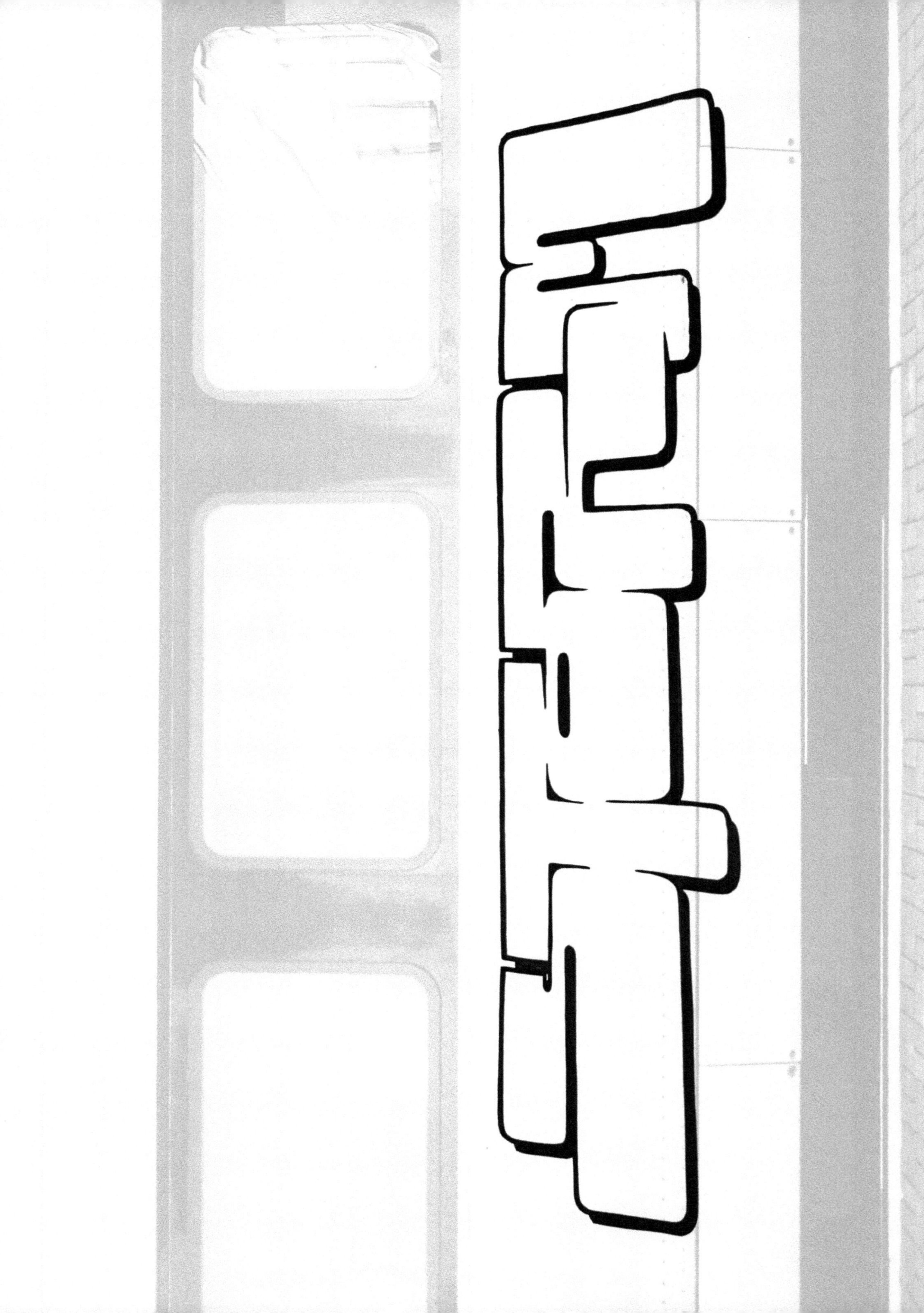

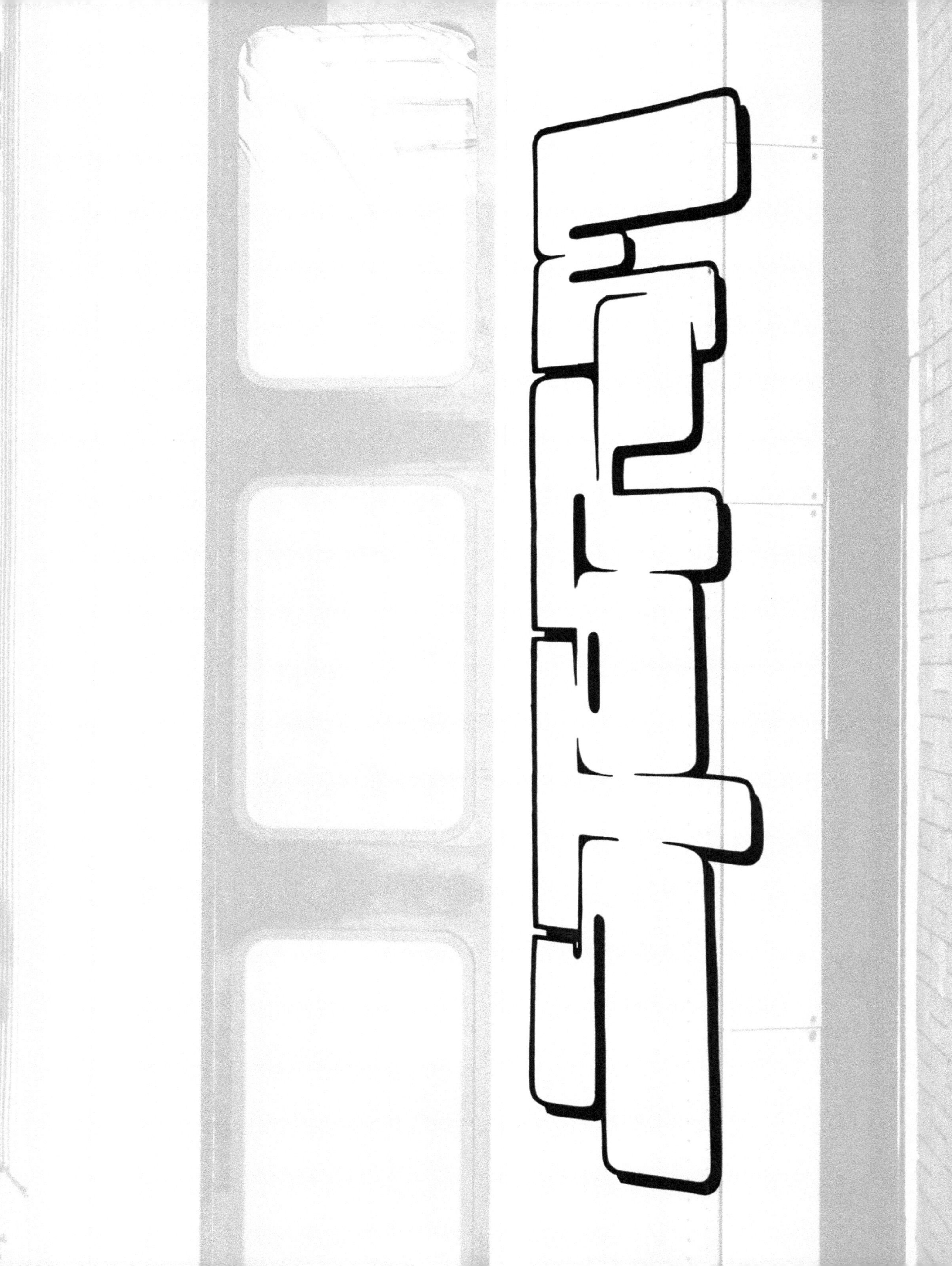

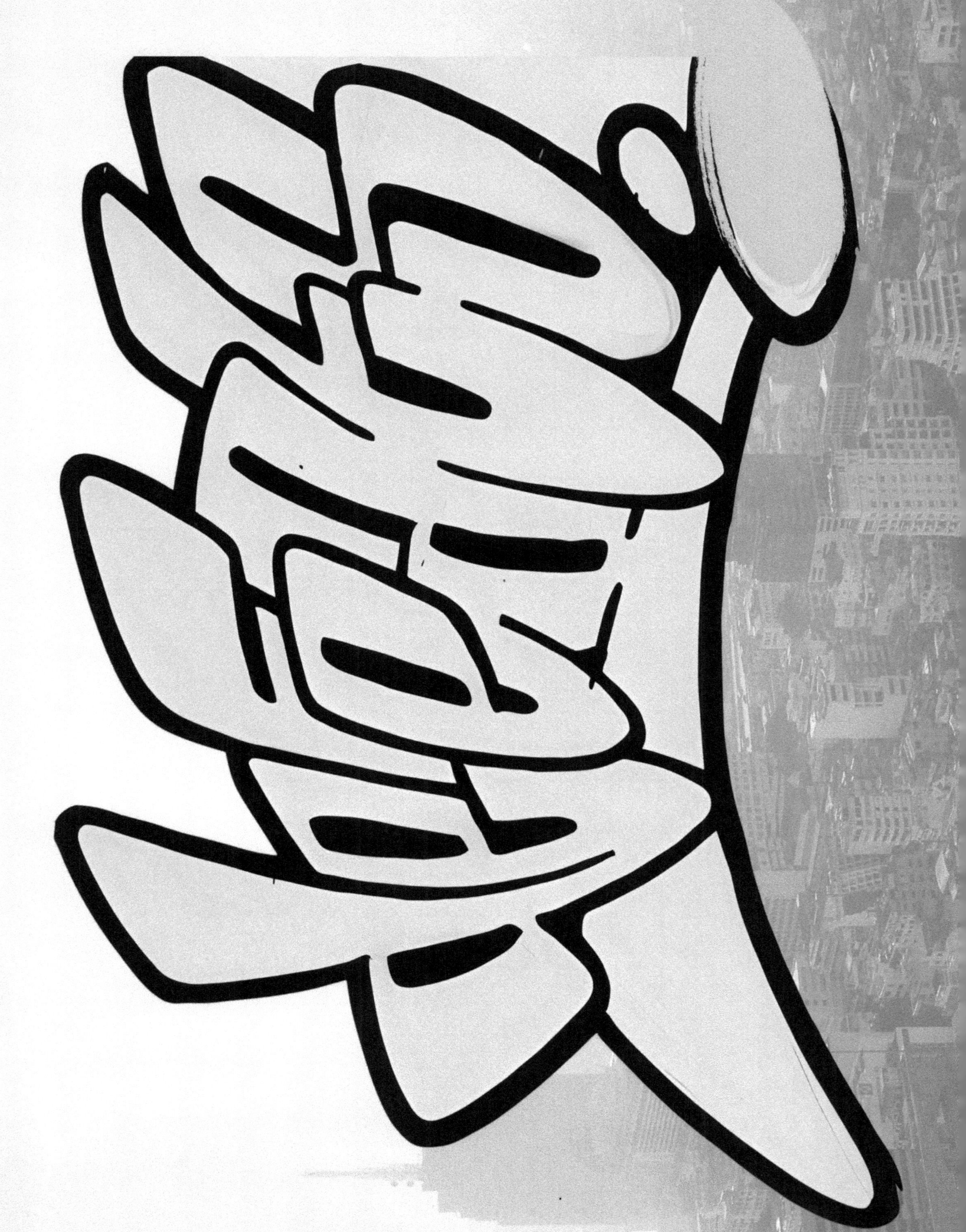

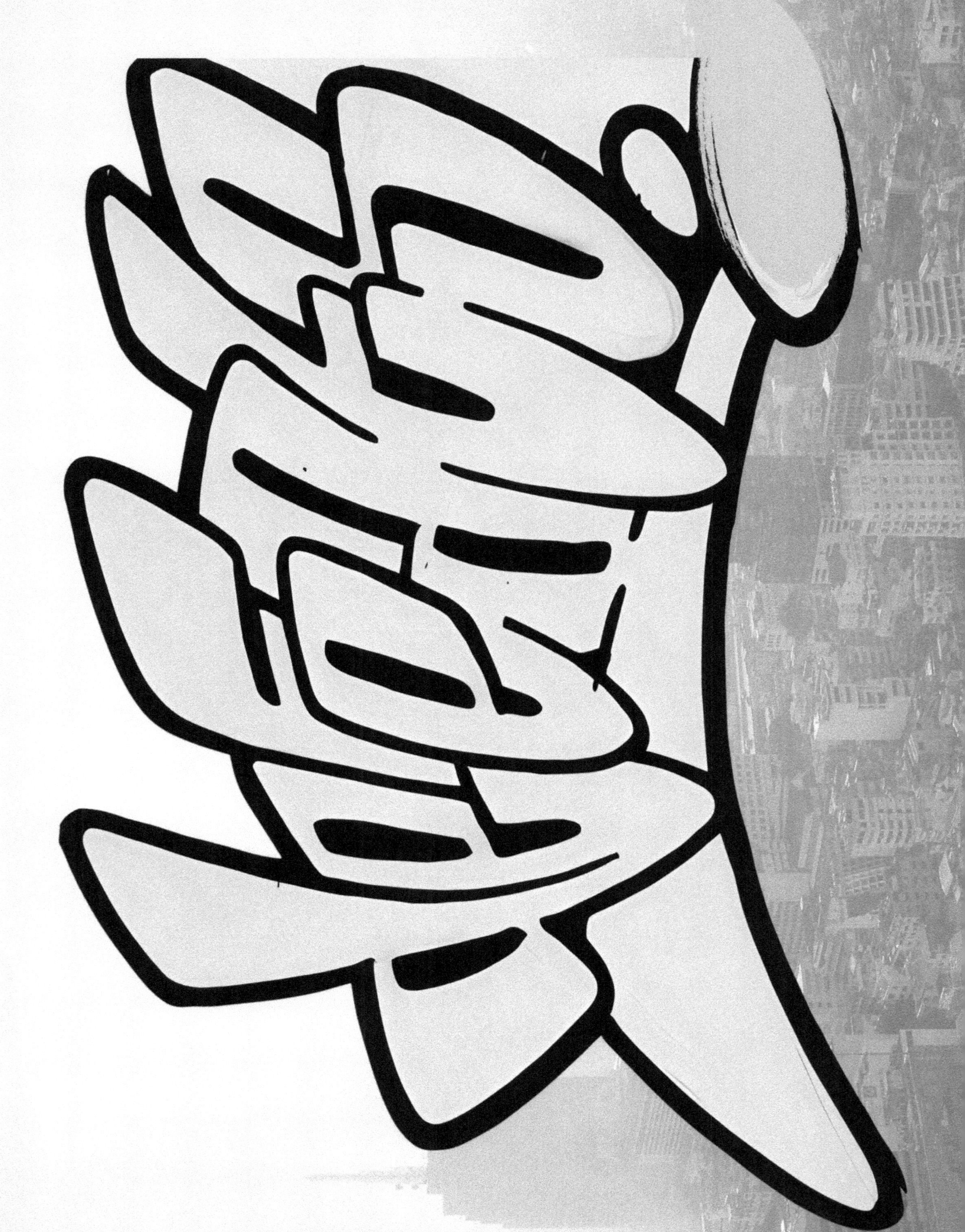

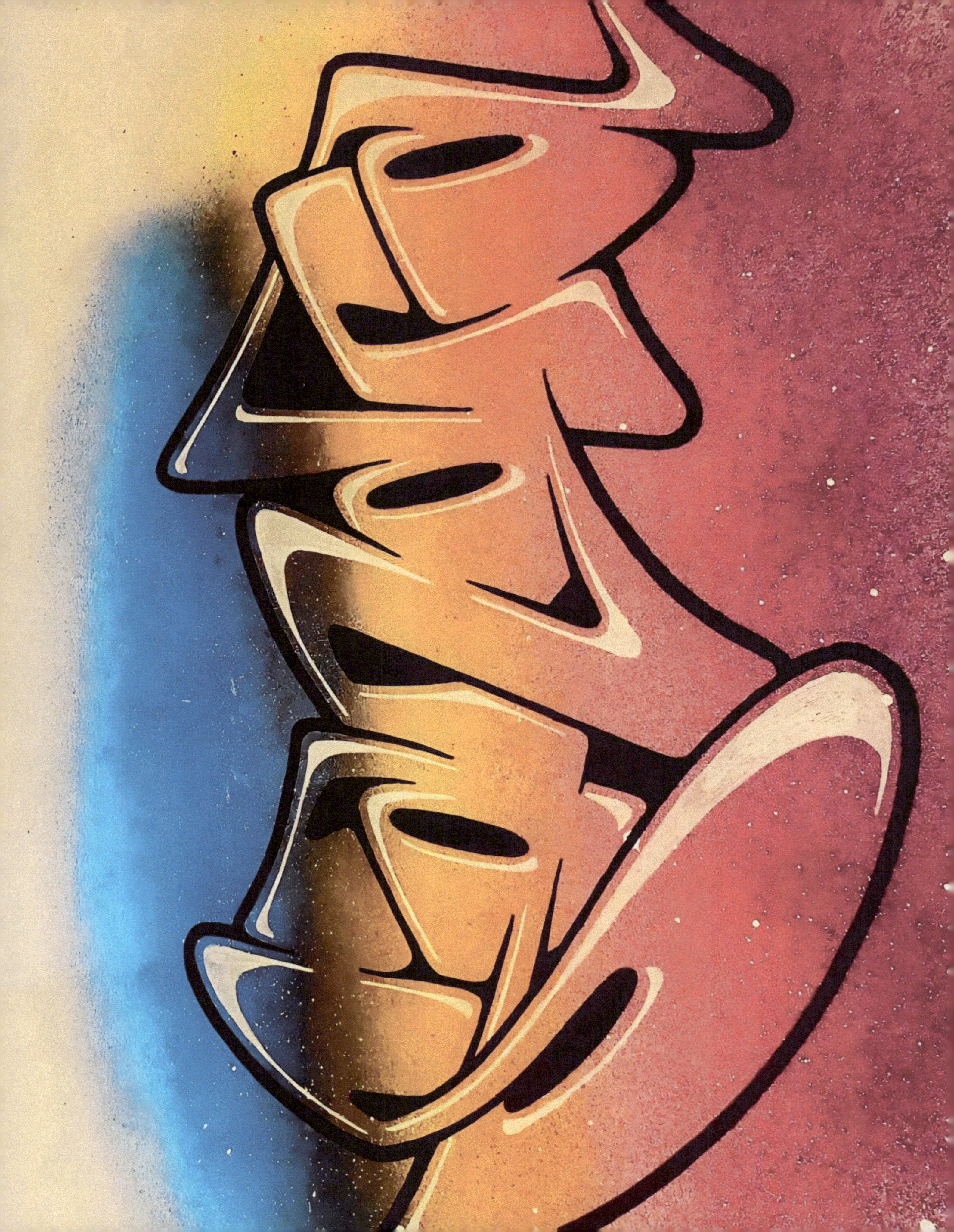

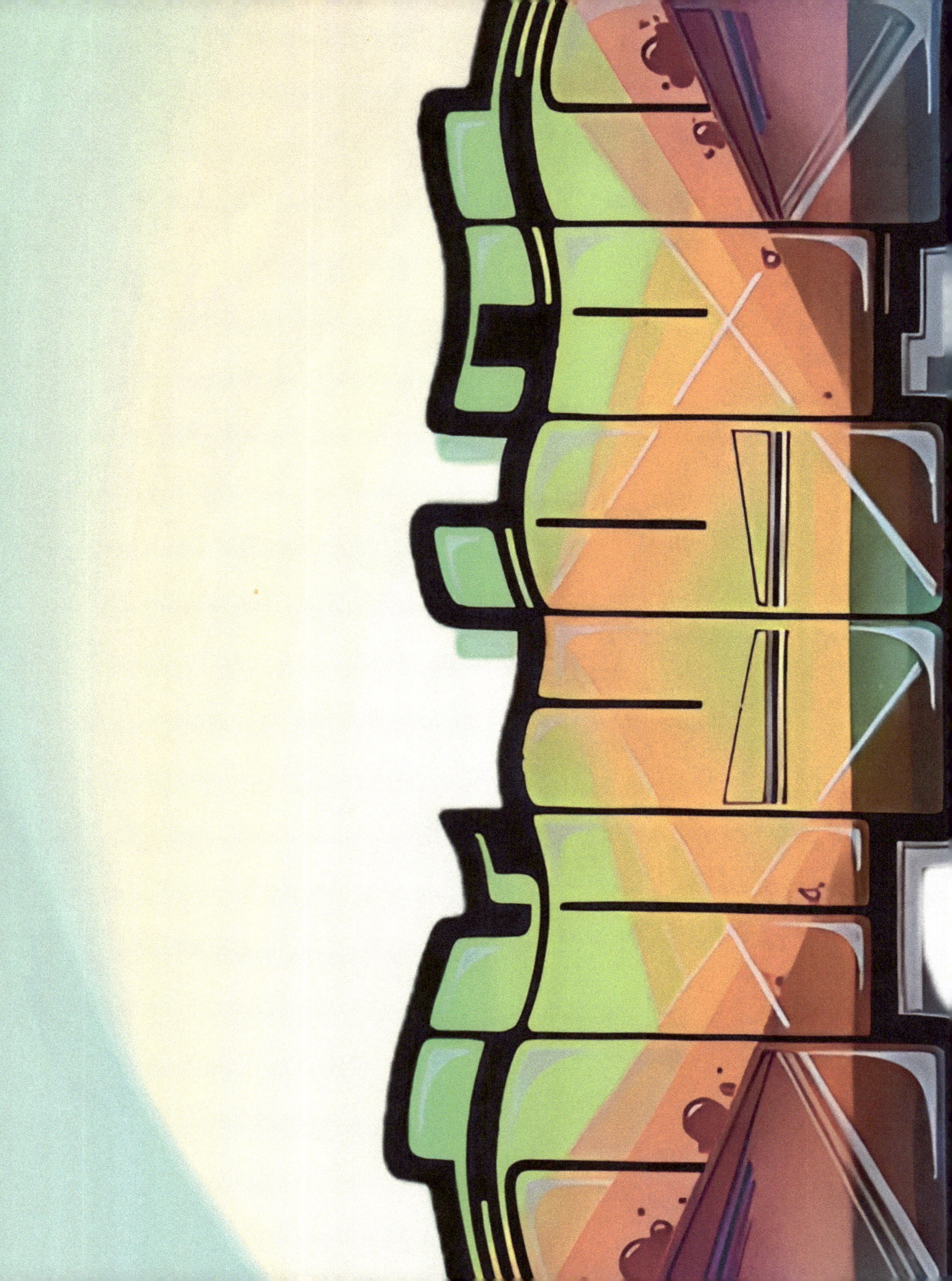

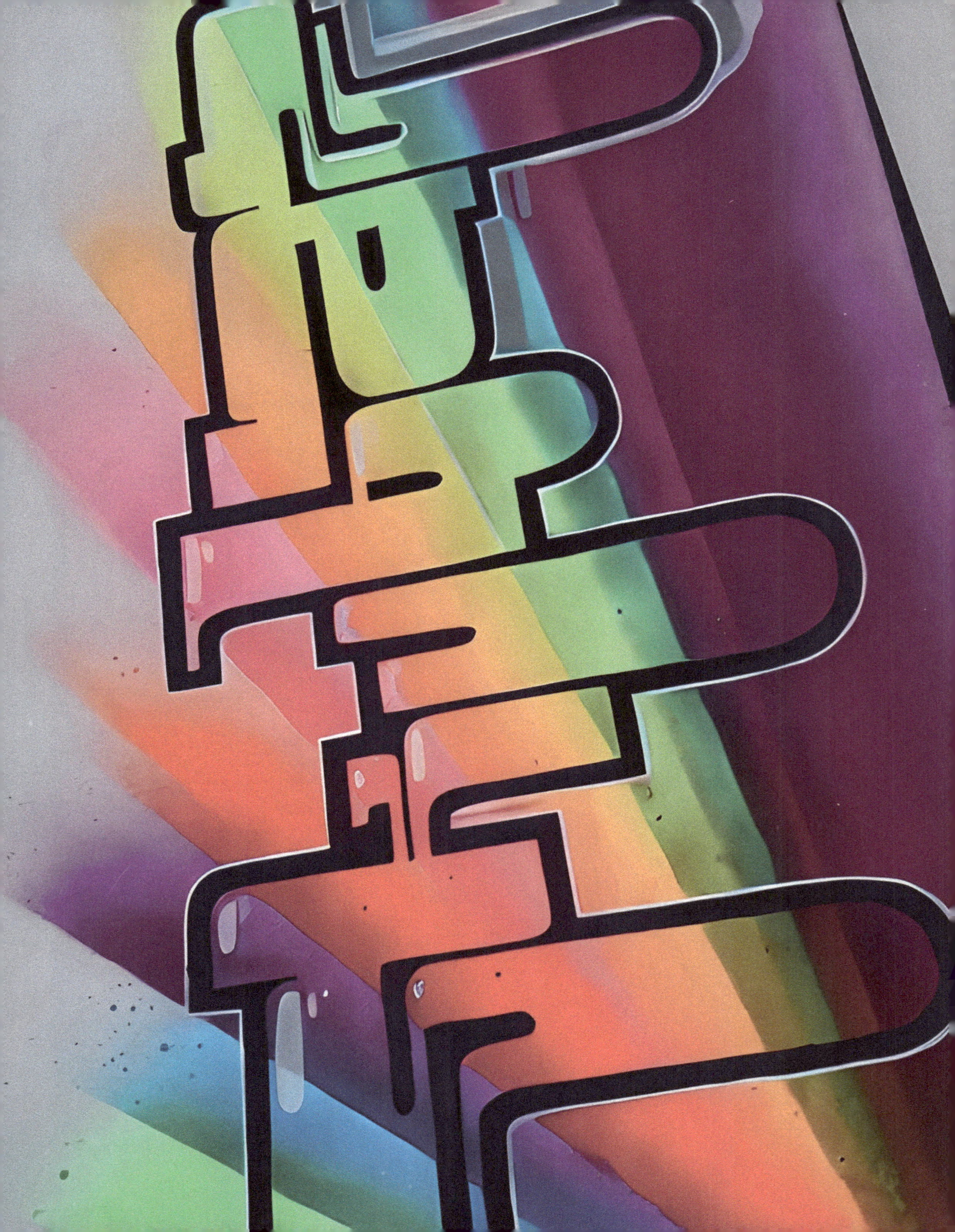

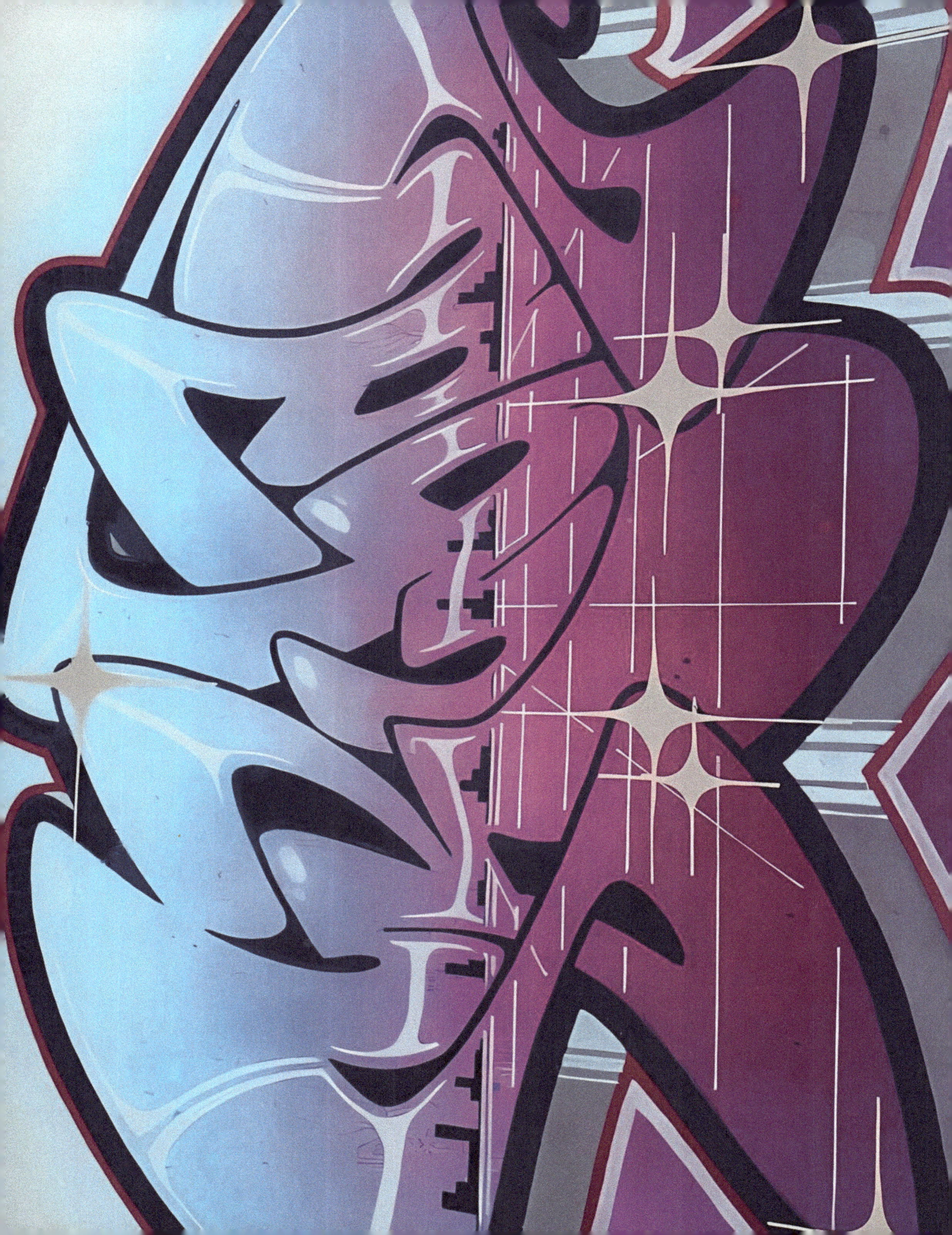

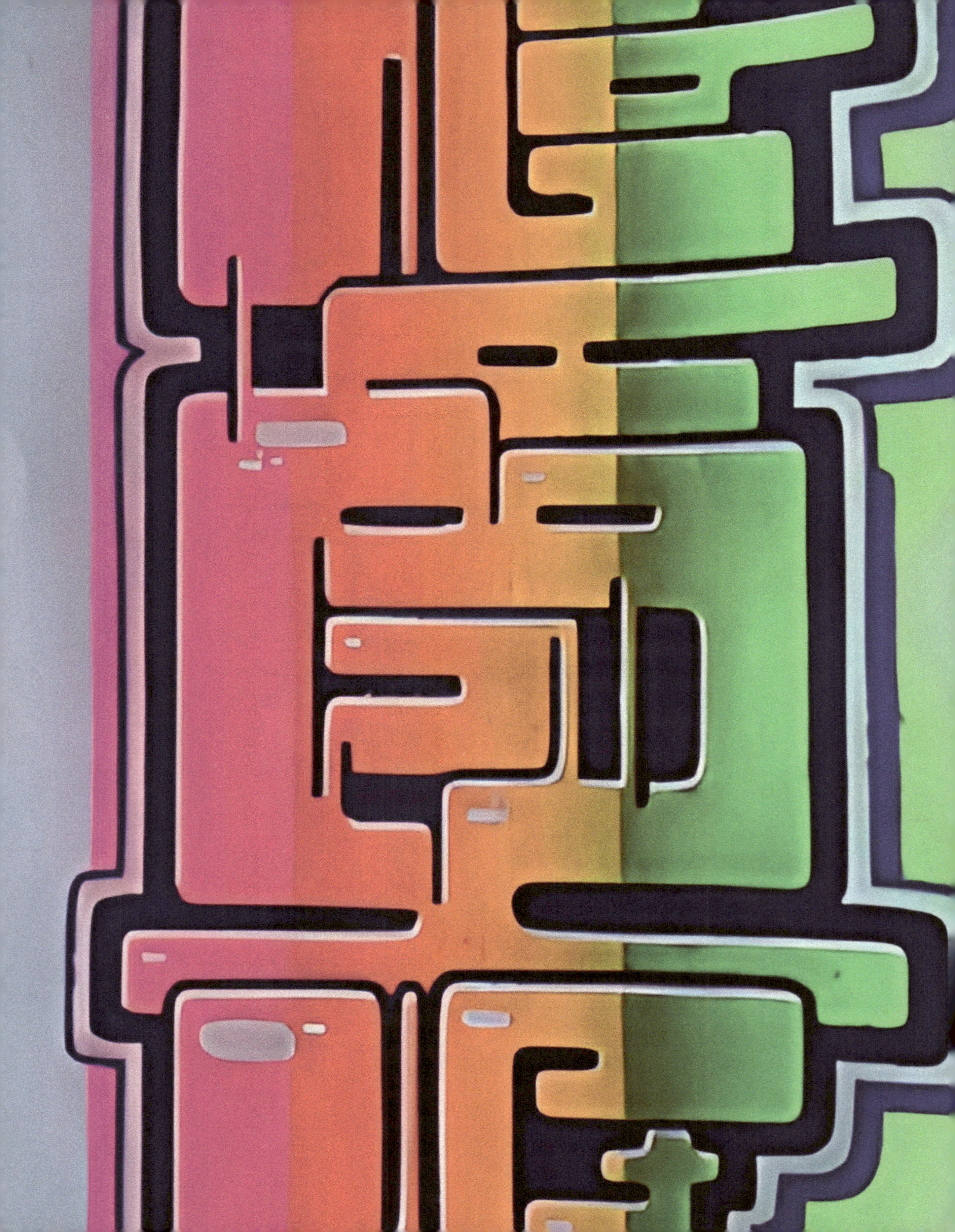

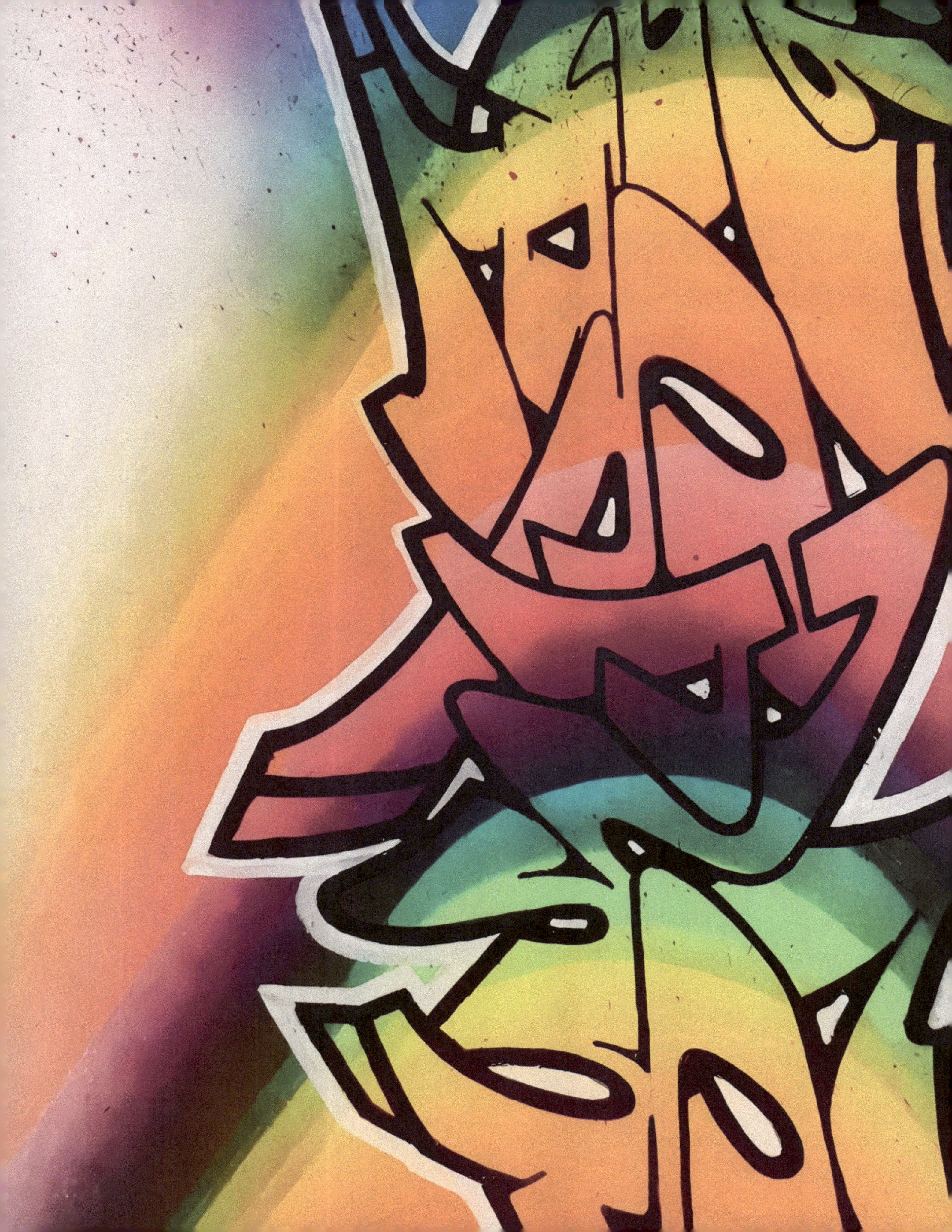

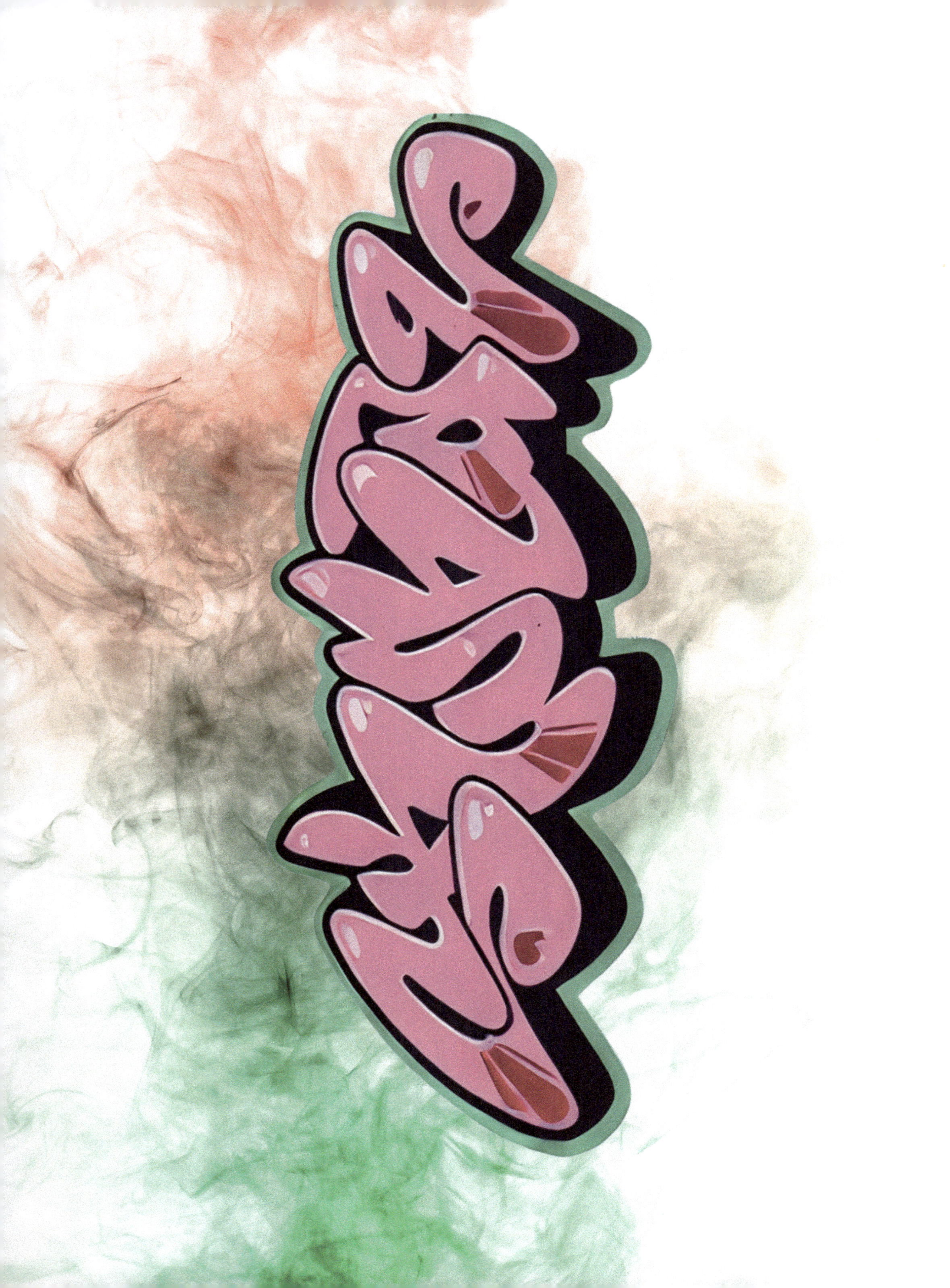

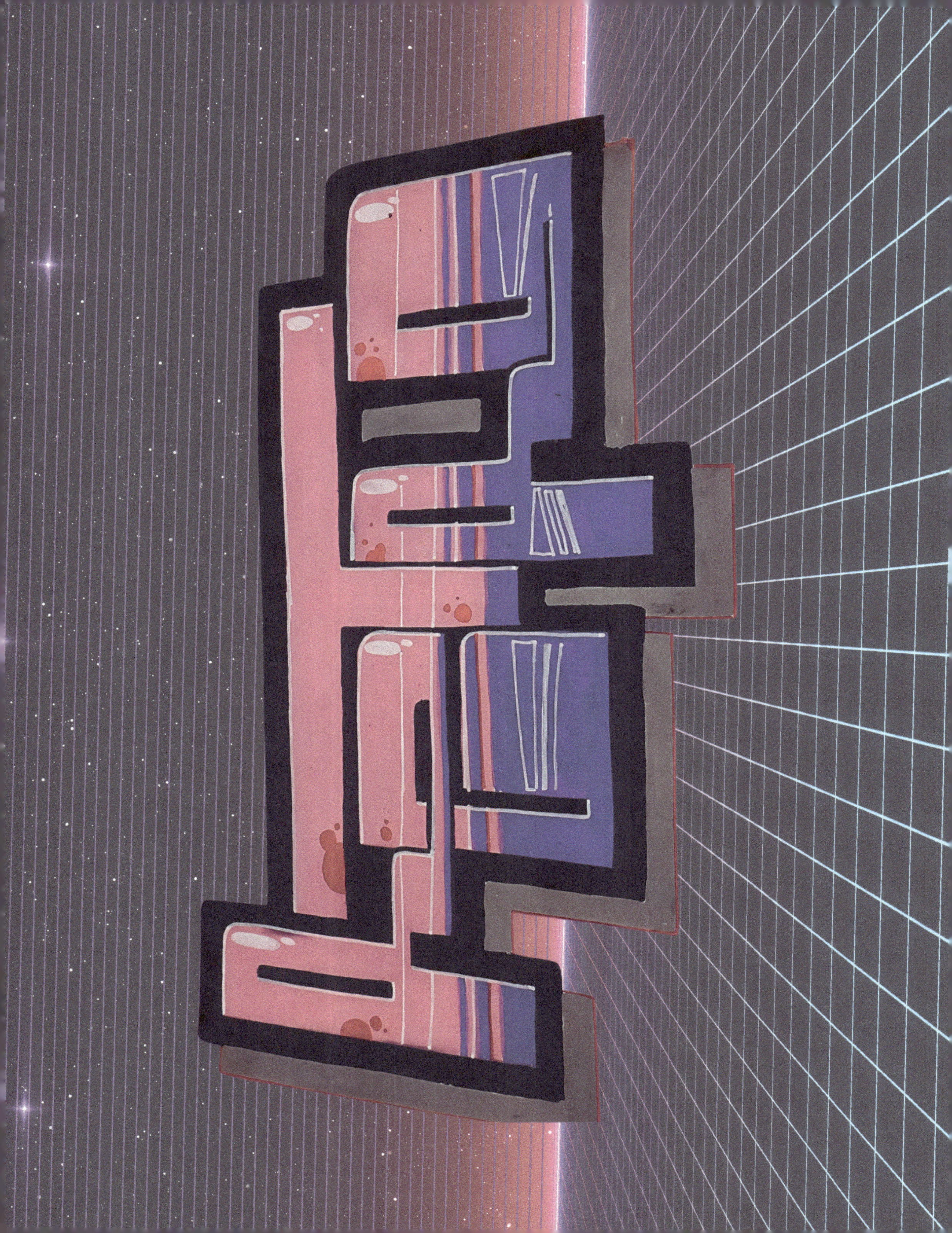

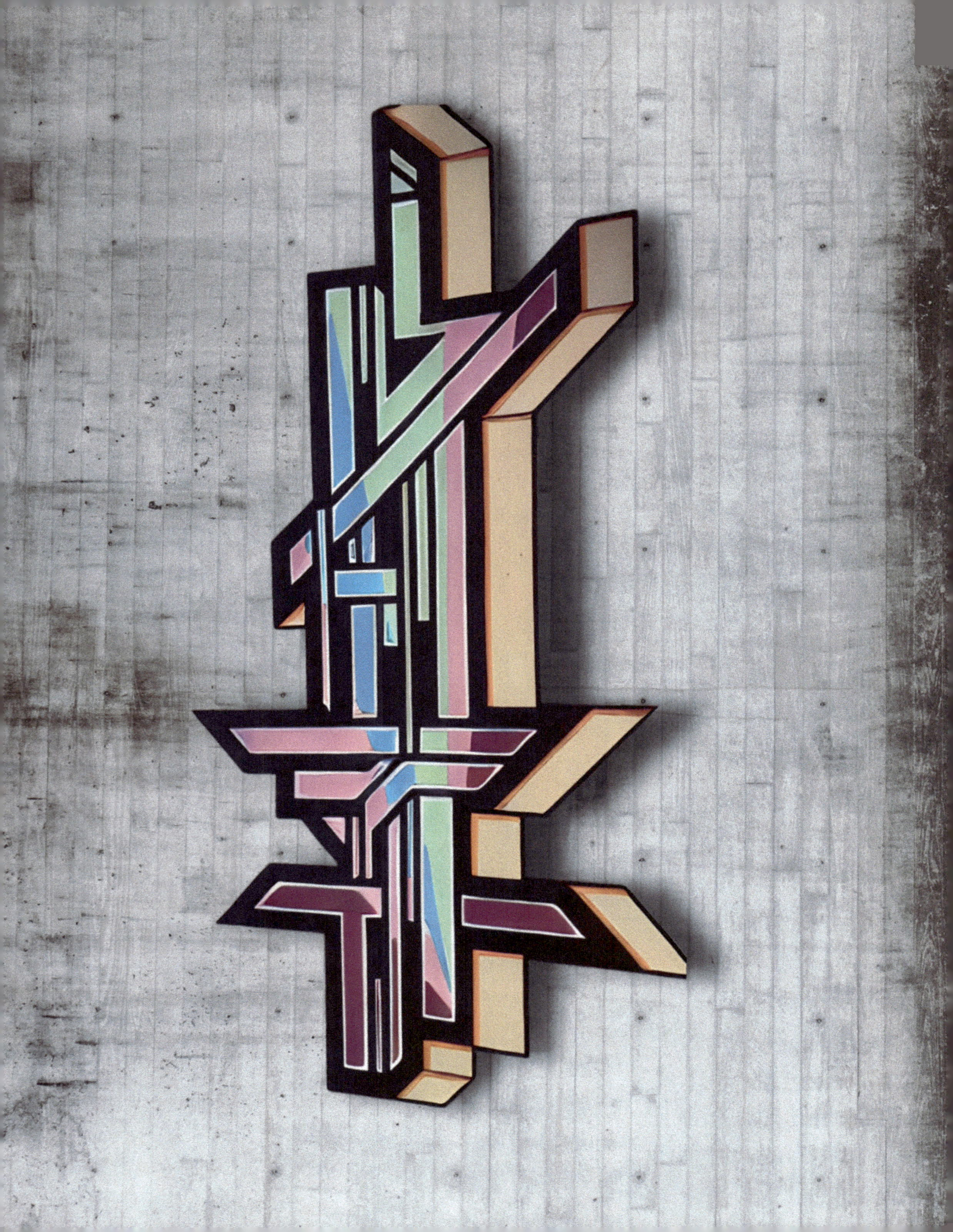

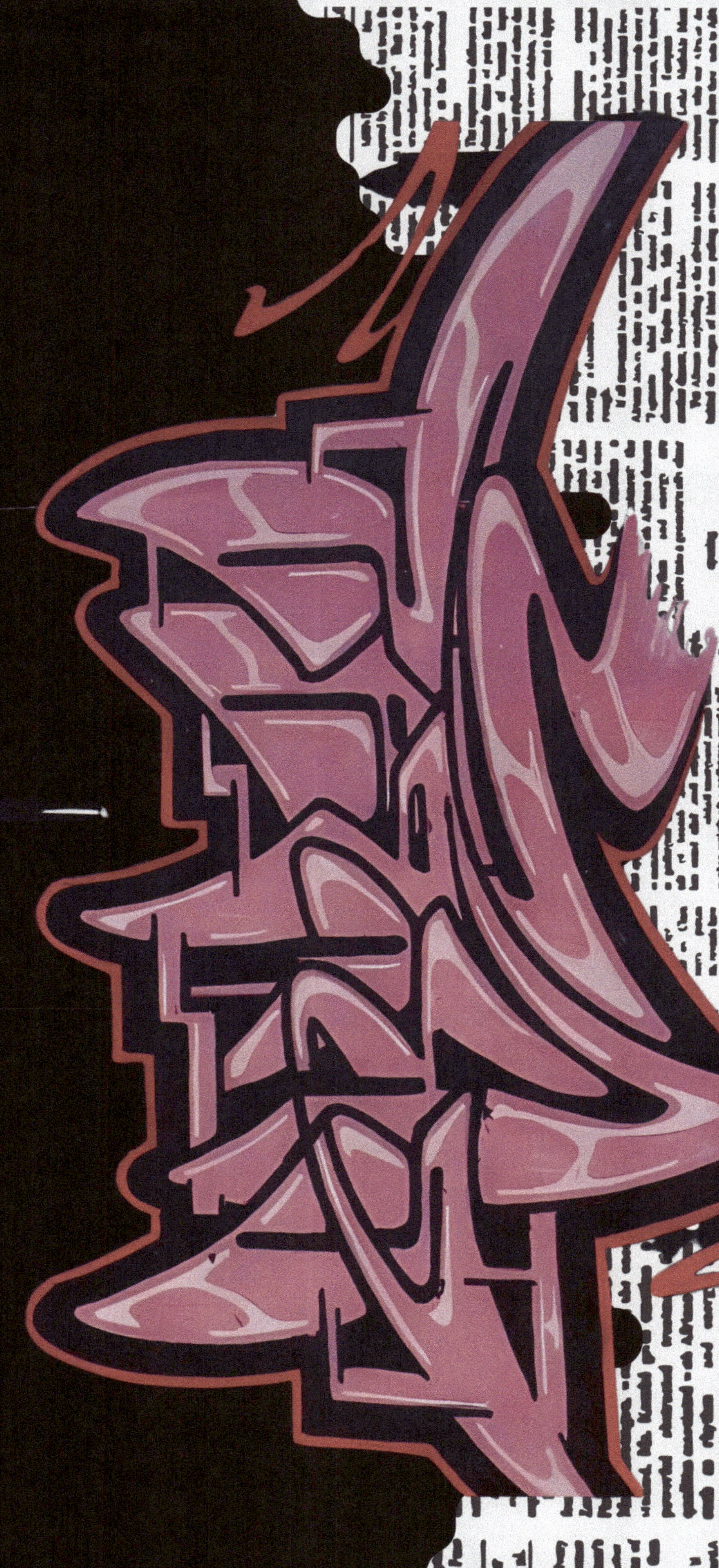

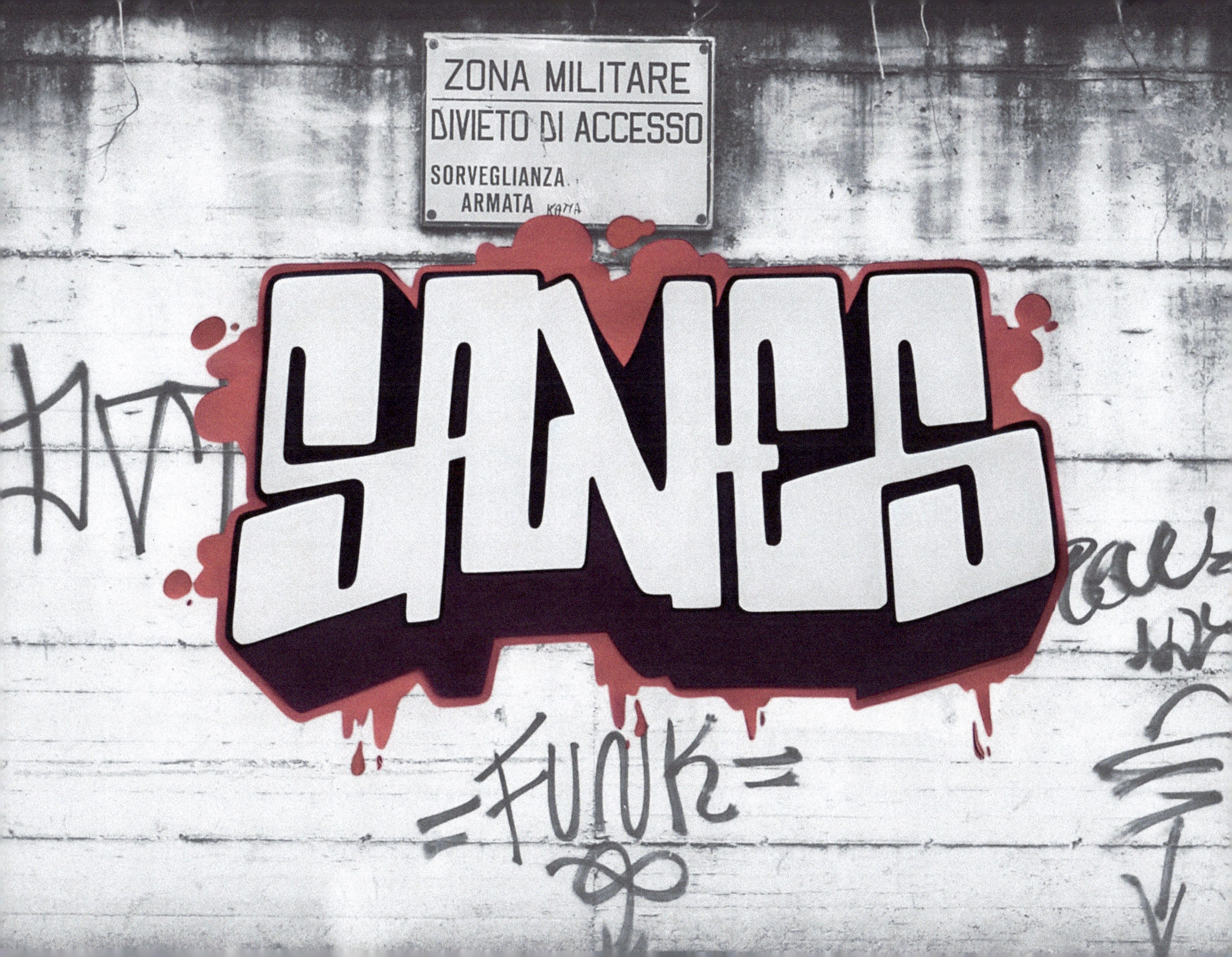

ZONA MILITARE
DIVIETO DI ACCESSO
SORVEGLIANZA
ARMATA

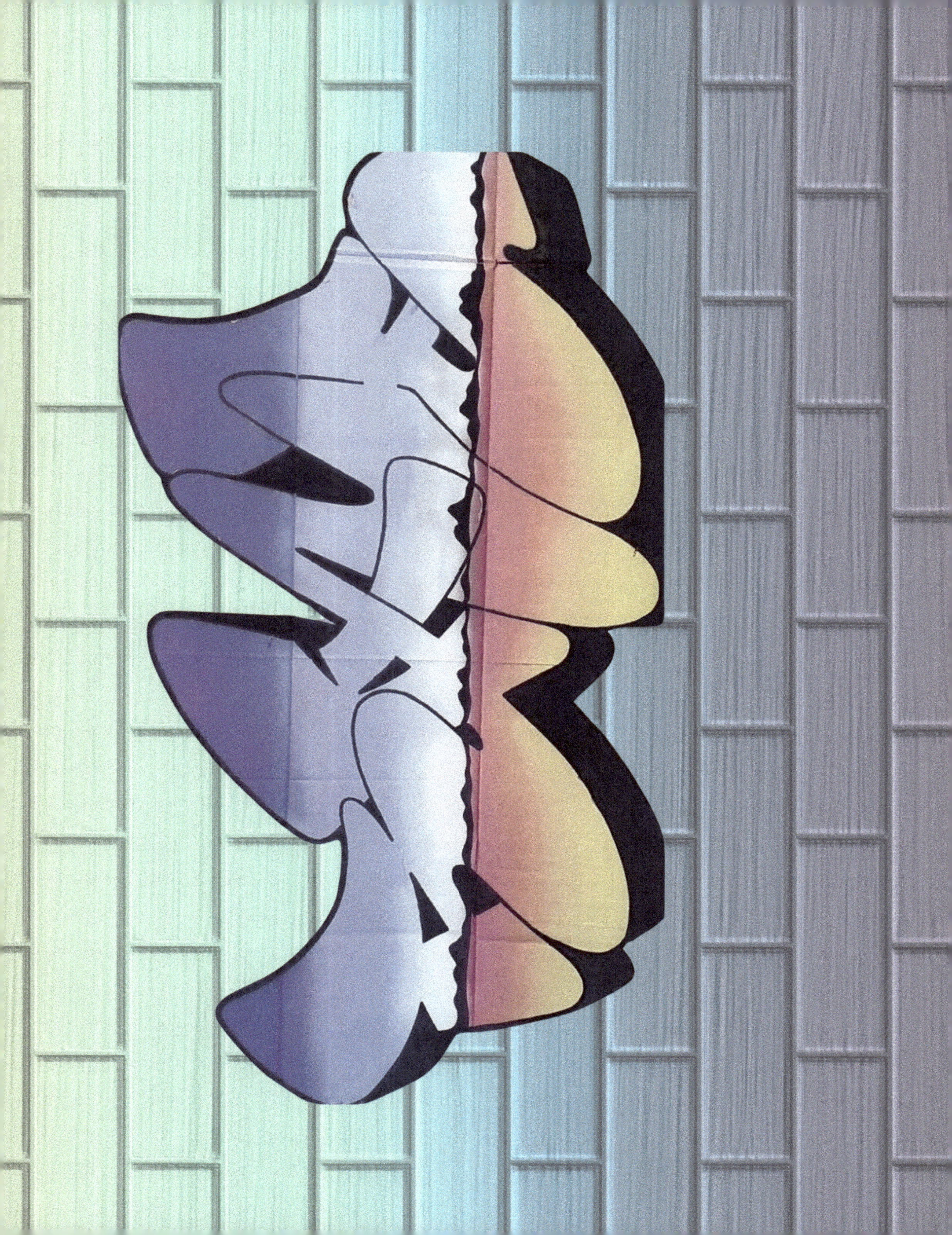

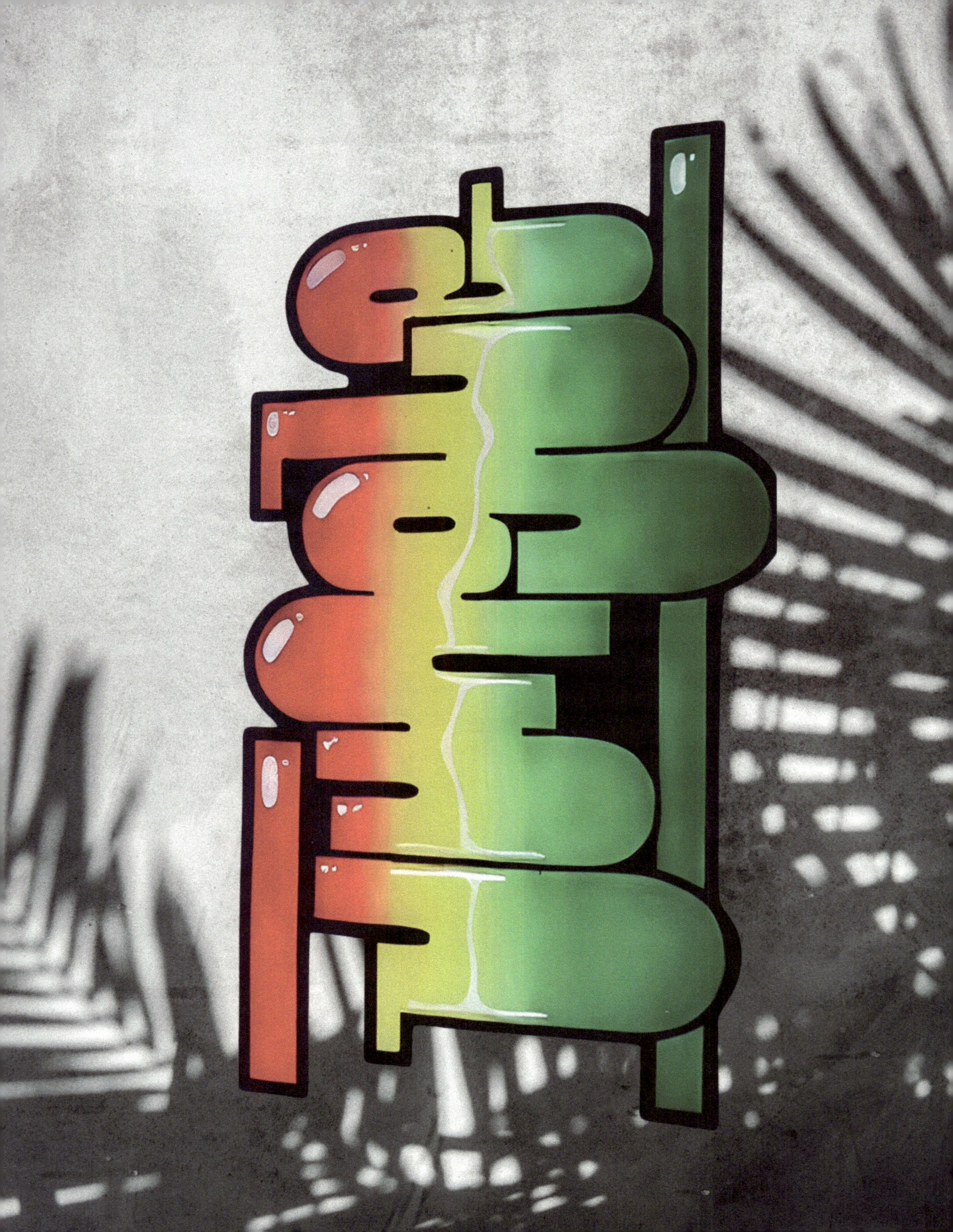

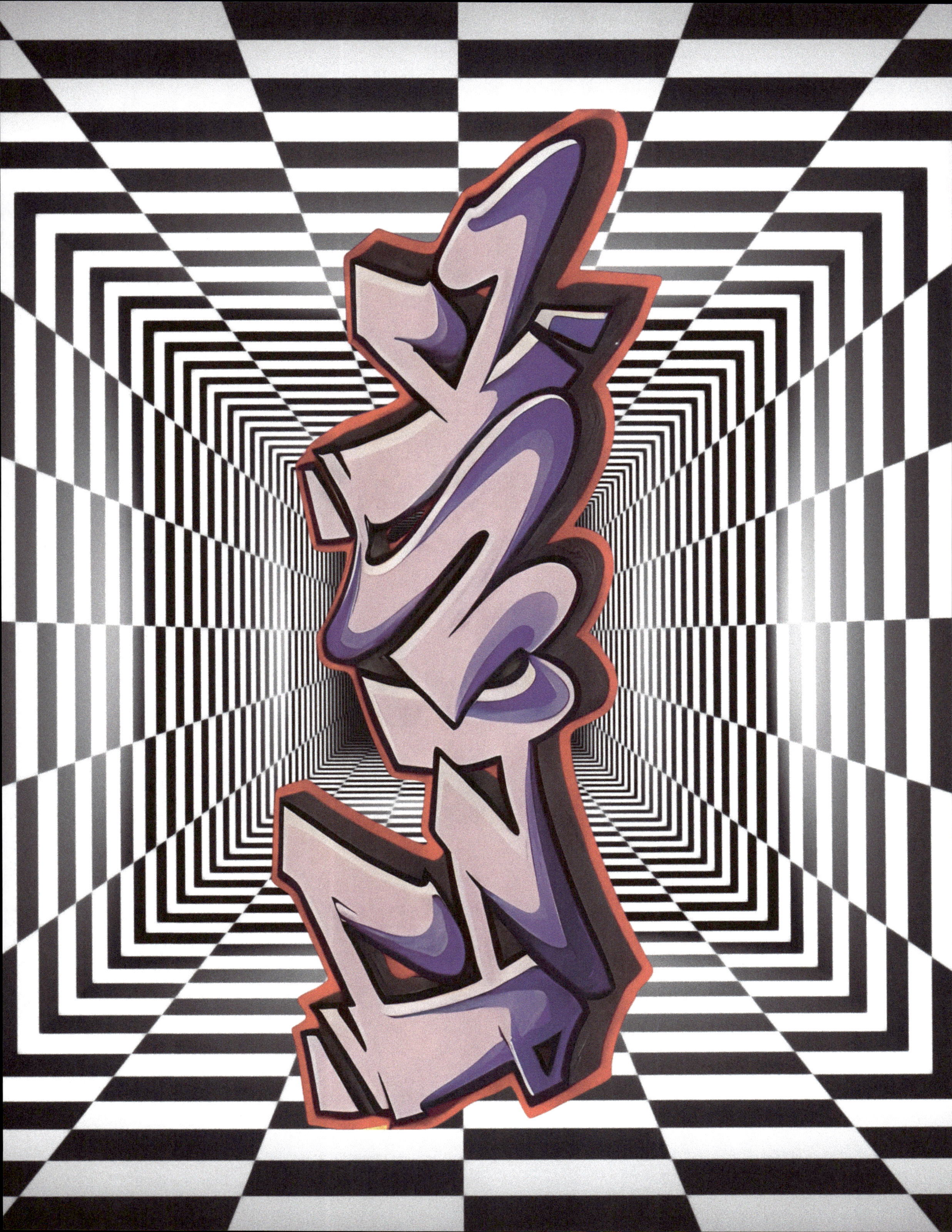

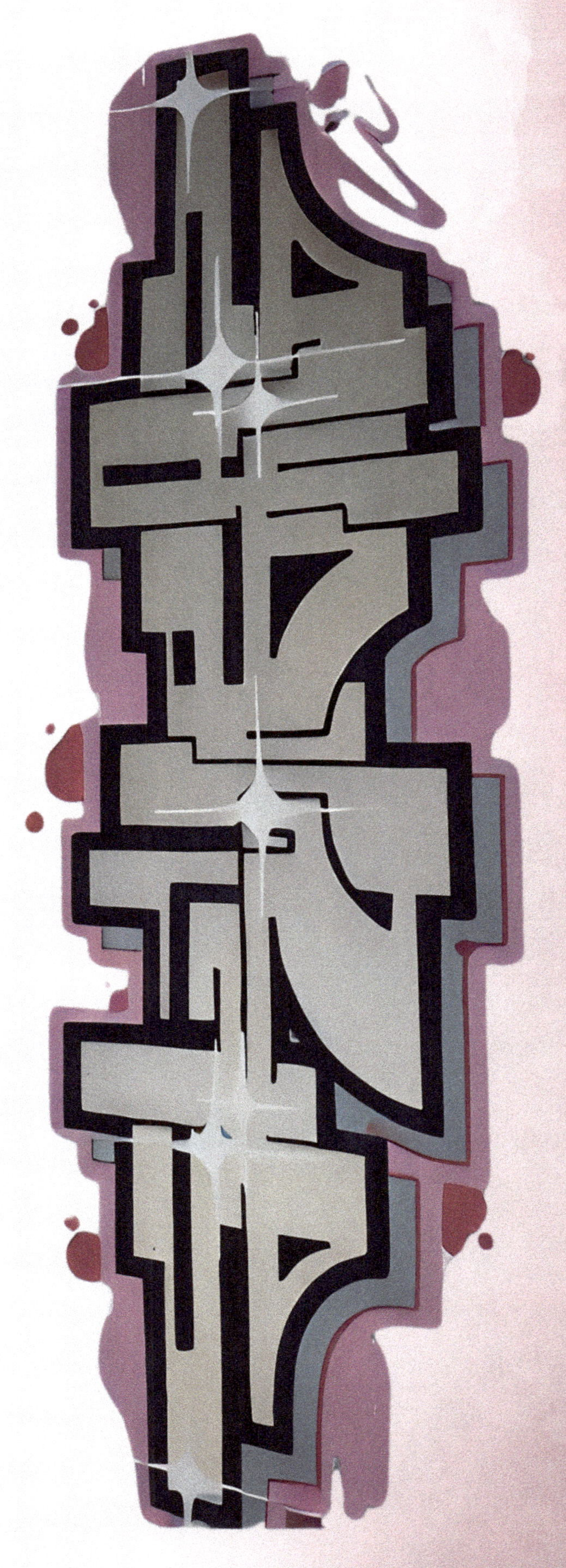

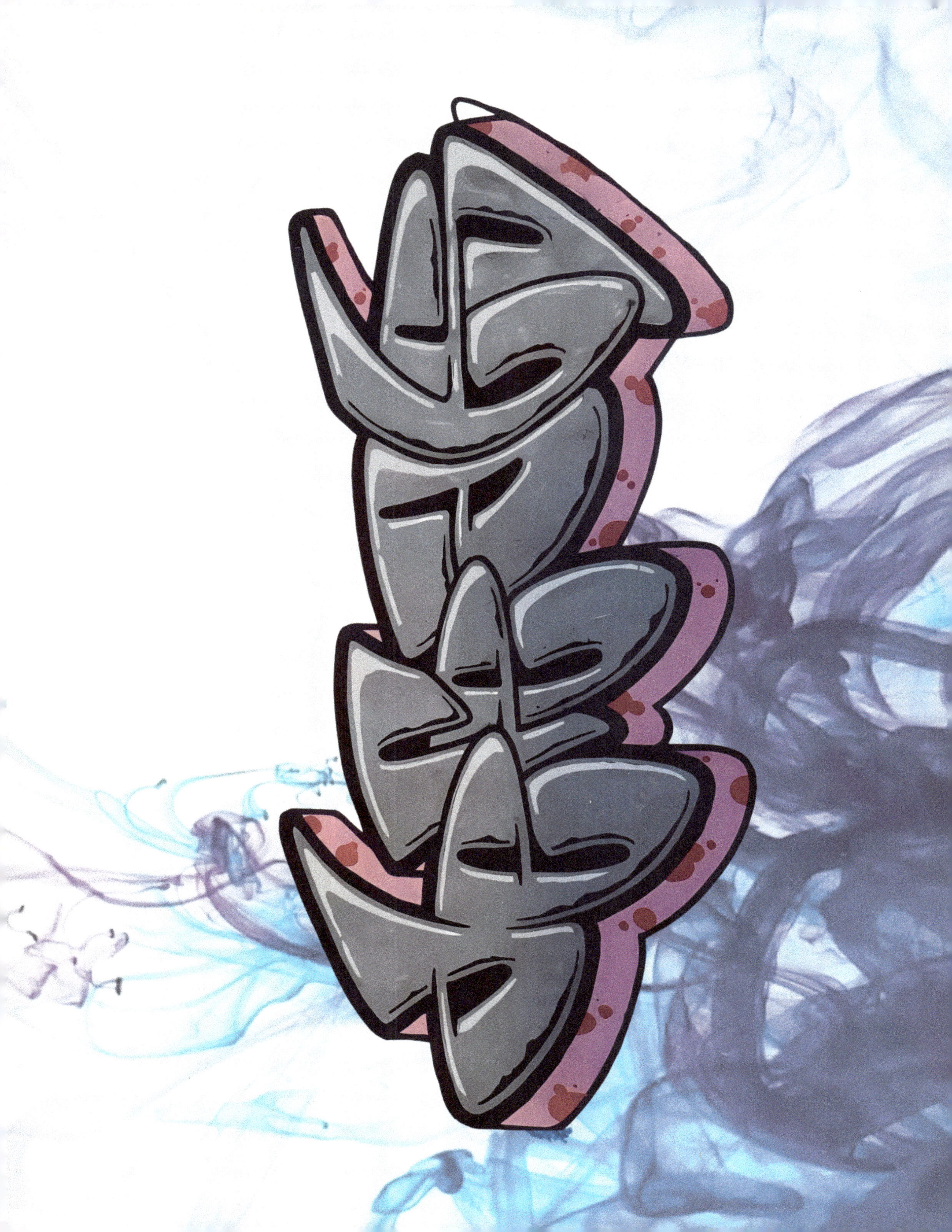

SHADING & SHADOWS

BEGIN WITH THE LETTER "A," IMAGINING LIGHT SHINING FROM THE TOP RIGHT. THE LEFT SIDE OF THE "A" WILL APPEAR DARKER, WHILE THE RIGHT SIDE WILL BE ILLUMINATED, CREATING A SENSE OF DEPTH. THIS MIMICS THE WAY SHADOWS NATURALLY FALL ON LETTERS WHEN LIT FROM ONE SIDE. THIS TECHNIQUE CAN BE APPLIED TO ALL LETTERS.

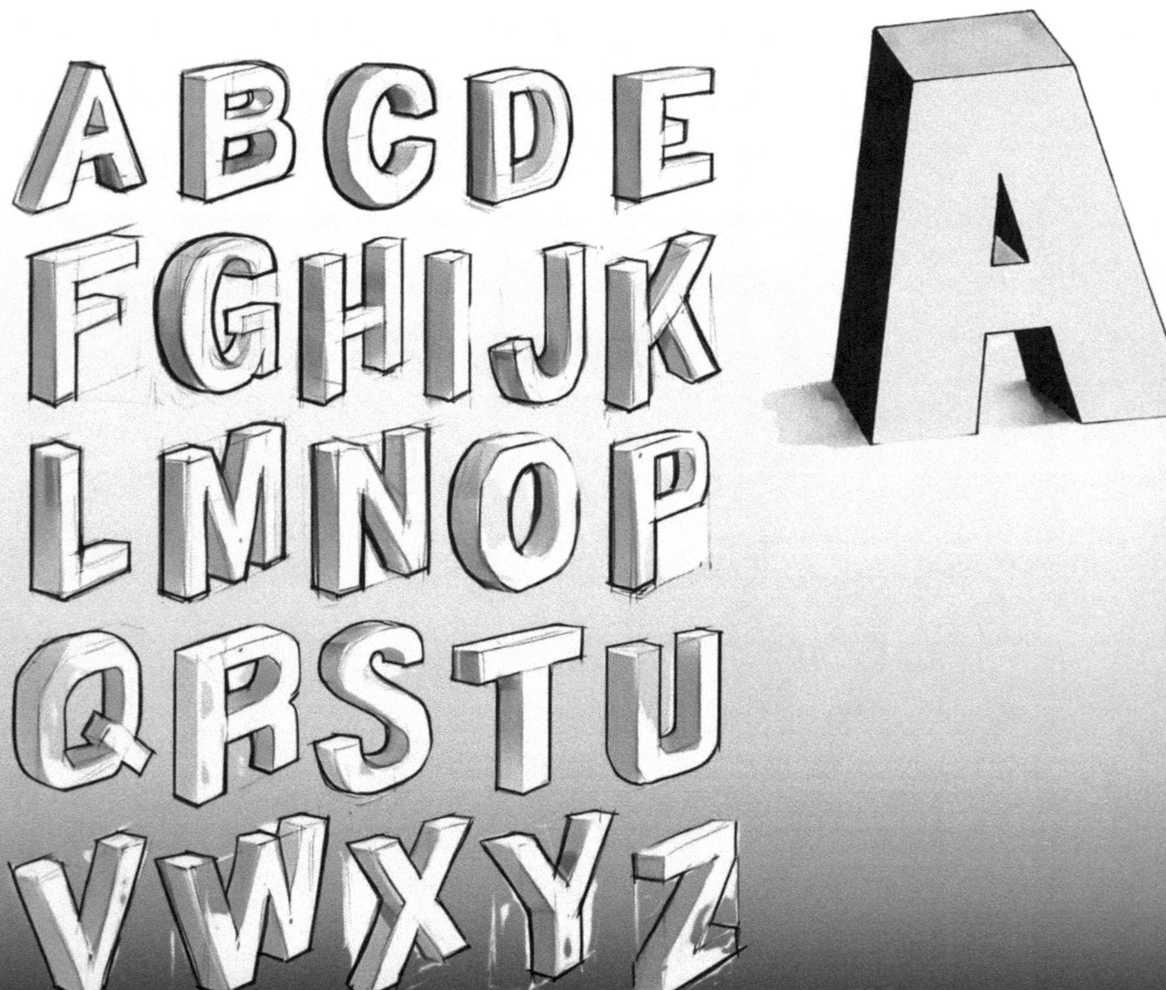

A B C D E
F G H I J K
L M N O P
Q R S T U
V W X Y Z
A

<u>COLOR BLENDING</u>

TRANSITIONING FROM PINK AT THE TOP TO GREEN AT THE BOTTOM. LOOK FOR IMAGES WHERE THE TWO COLORS MIX SEAMLESSLY, JUST LIKE BLENDING TWO SHADES WITHIN THE SAME LETTER TO CREATE A SMOOTH GRADIENT EFFECT.

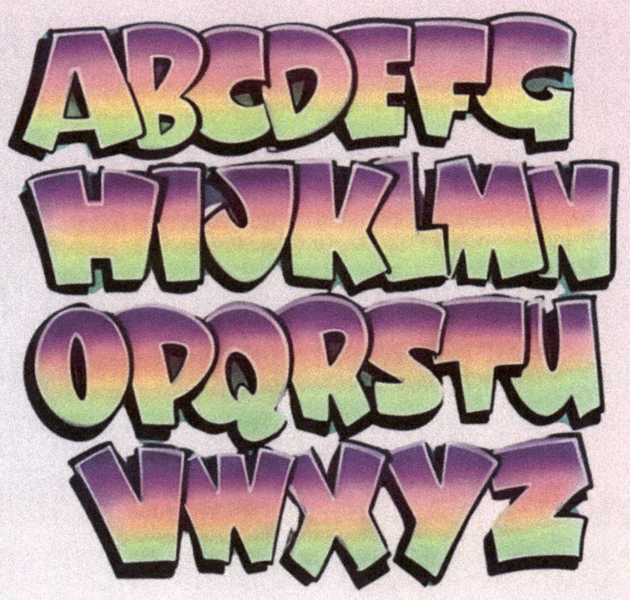

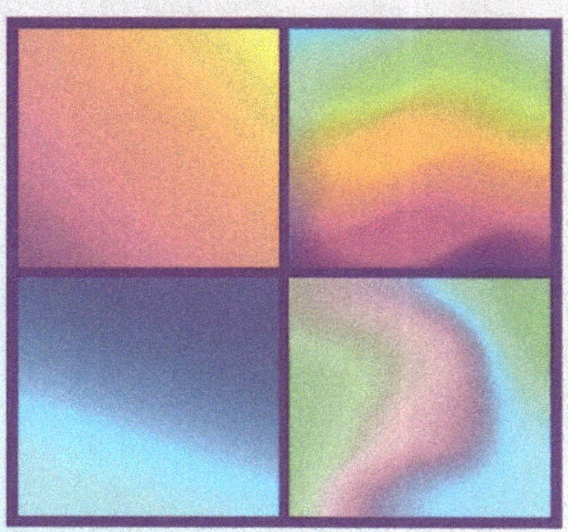

<u>OUTLINING</u>

TO CREATE A BOLD LOOK START WITH A THICK, DARK OUTLINE. THIS BORDER DISTINCTLY SHAPES THE LETTER, HELPING IT STAND OUT. OPT FOR A DARKER PEN OR MARKER THAT CONTRASTS WITH THE FILL COLOR OF THE LETTER. TAKE YOUR TIME TO TRACE AROUND THE EDGES FOR AN EVEN OUTLINE. YOU MIGHT ALSO EXPERIMENT WITH VARIOUS STYLES, SUCH AS DASHED LINES, FOR A TOUCH OF CREATIVITY. A STRONG OUTLINE NOT ONLY BOOSTS VISIBILITY BUT ALSO IMPARTS A SENSE OF STRUCTURE TO THE LETTER. FOR ADDED DEPTH, THINK ABOUT INCORPORATING A LIGHTER OUTLINE AROUND THE DARK ONE TO ACHIEVE A SUBTLE LAYERED EFFECT.

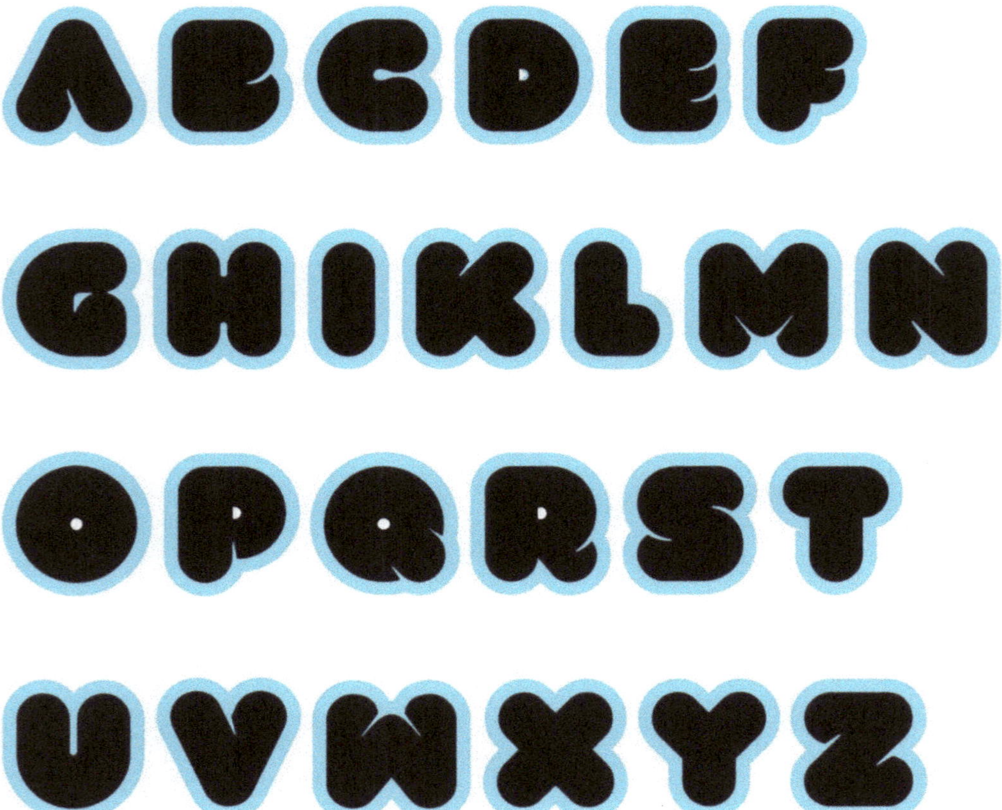

TEXTURES

VISUALIZE THE LETTER "M" WITH A ROUGH TEXTURE USING STIPPLING AND CROSS-HATCHING TECHNIQUES. STIPPLING INVOLVES SMALL DOTS TO CREATE SHADOW AND DEPTH, WHILE CROSS-HATCHING USES OVERLAPPING LINES IN DIFFERENT DIRECTIONS TO DEPICT TEXTURE AND LIGHT. VARYING THE DENSITY OF DOTS OR LINES ENHANCES THE TACTILE QUALITY, WITH DARKER AREAS INDICATING DETAIL AND LIGHTER AREAS SUGGESTING REFLECTIONS.

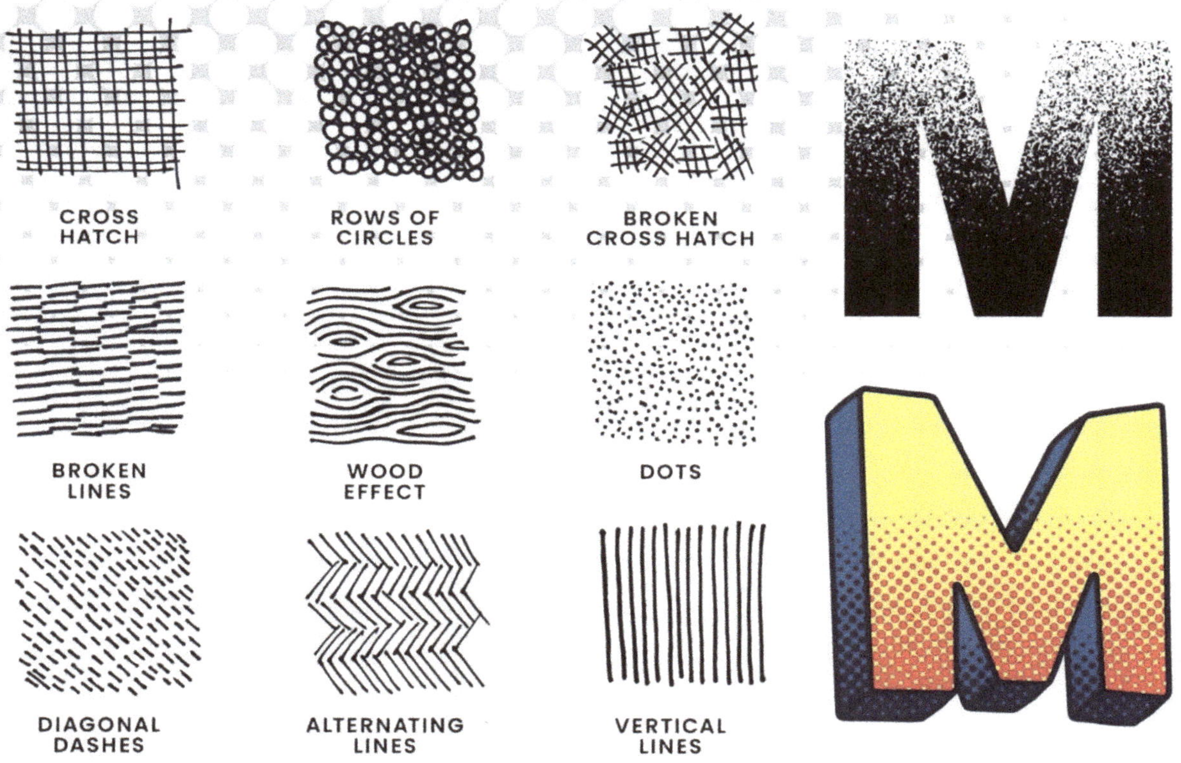

CROSS HATCH

ROWS OF CIRCLES

BROKEN CROSS HATCH

BROKEN LINES

WOOD EFFECT

DOTS

DIAGONAL DASHES

ALTERNATING LINES

VERTICAL LINES

<u>LIGHT SOURCE</u>

WHEN LIGHT SHINES FROM ABOVE ON THE LETTER "C," THE TOP EDGE WILL APPEAR BRIGHT DUE TO THE HIGHLIGHT, WHILE THE BOTTOM AND INNER AREAS WILL BE DARKER, CREATING SHADOWS. THIS CONTRAST BETWEEN LIGHT AND DARK ADDS DEPTH, MAKING THE LETTER LOOK THREE-DIMENSIONAL.

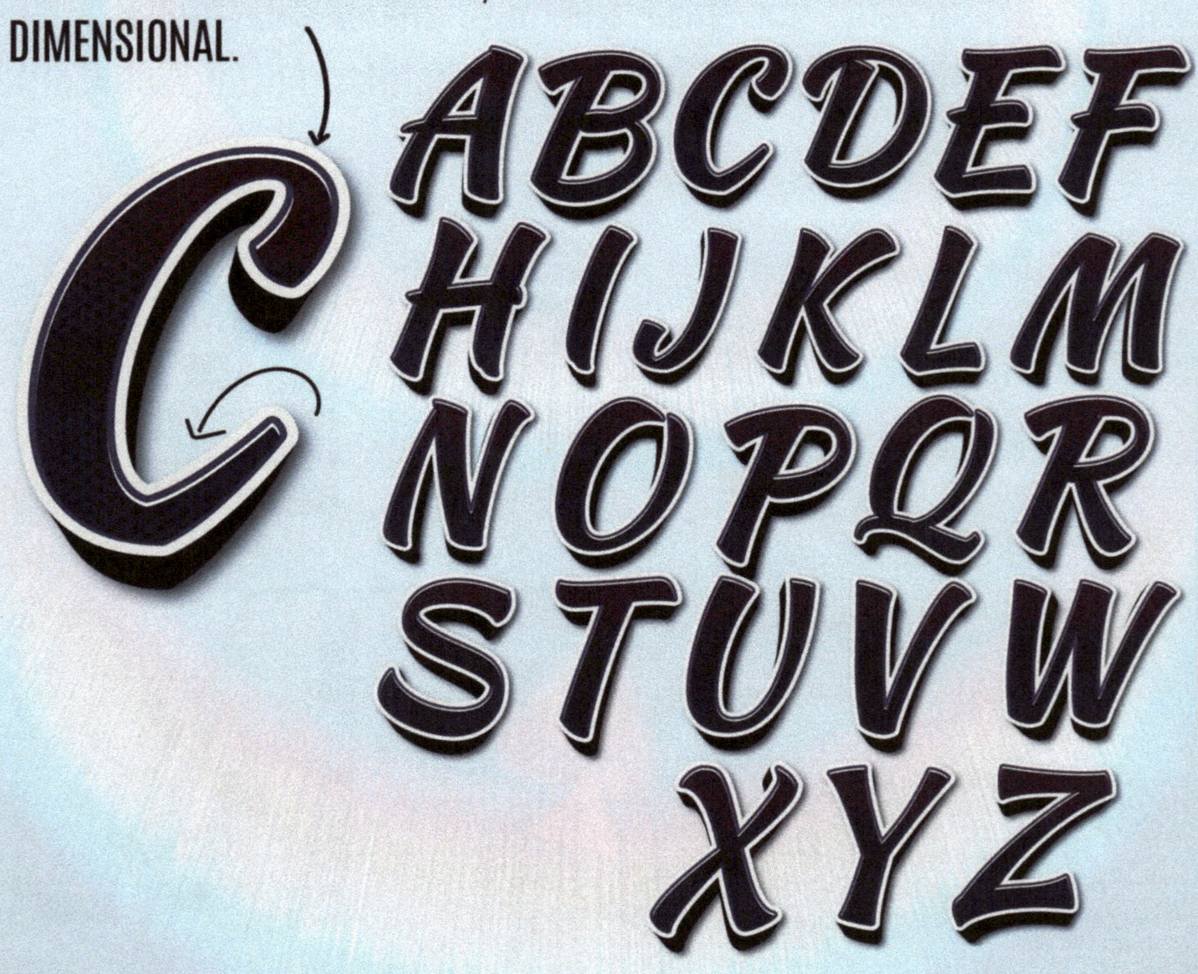

<u>COLORS CHOICES</u>

COMPLEMENTARY COLORS: OPT FOR COLORS THAT ARE OPPOSITE EACH OTHER ON THE COLOR WHEEL (E.G., BLUE AND ORANGE) TO ACHIEVE A VIBRANT CONTRAST.

ANALOGOUS COLORS: CHOOSE COLORS THAT SIT NEXT TO EACH OTHER ON THE WHEEL (E.G., BLUE, BLUE-GREEN, GREEN) FOR A HARMONIOUS AND CALMING EFFECT.

TRIADIC COLORS: SELECT THREE COLORS THAT ARE EVENLY SPACED AROUND THE COLOR WHEEL (E.G., RED, YELLOW, BLUE) FOR A BALANCED YET LIVELY APPEARANCE.

MONOCHROMATIC: UTILIZE VARIOUS SHADES AND TINTS OF A SINGLE COLOR TO CREATE A COHESIVE AND SOPHISTICATED LOOK.
FEEL FREE TO EXPERIMENT WITH THESE COMBINATIONS, ADJUSTING SATURATION AND BRIGHTNESS TO DISCOVER WHAT RESONATES BEST WITH YOUR ARTWORK.

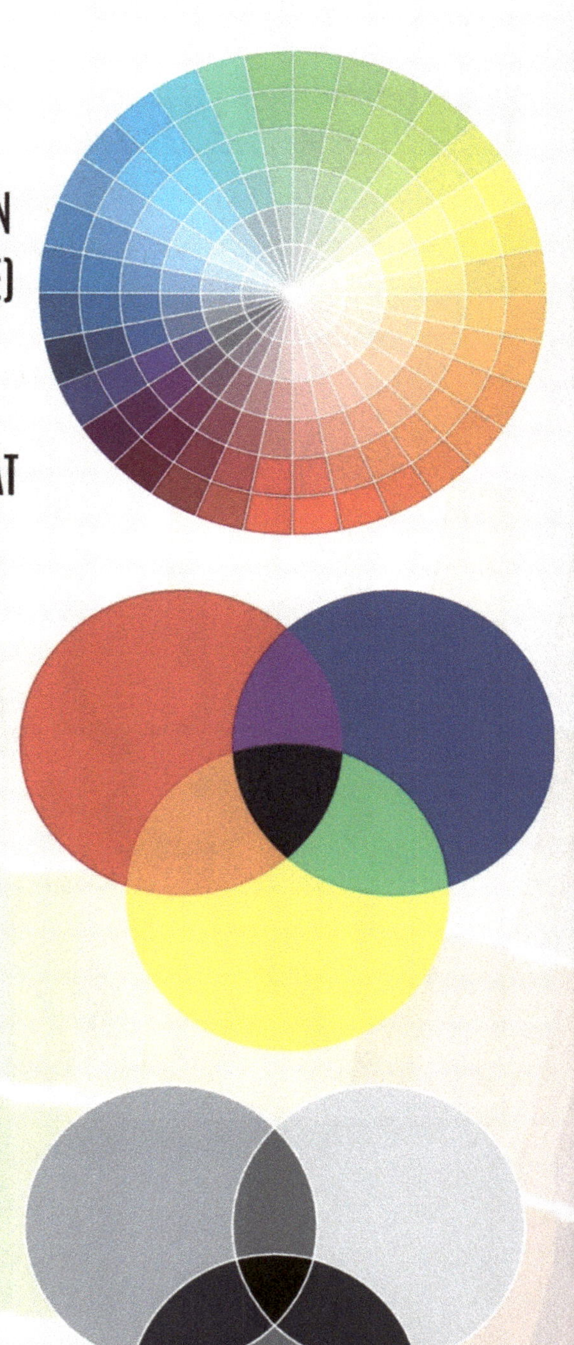

BASIC 3D ALPHABET

CREATE YOUR OWN PIECES.

AS YOU REACH THE FINAL PAGES OF THIS BOOK, IT'S TIME TO APPLY YOUR SKILLS AND EXPLORE YOUR OWN CREATIVE VISION. THIS BOOK HAS PROVIDED AN OPPORTUNITY TO EXAMINE THE STRUCTURE AND TECHNIQUES OF GRAFFITI ART, AND NOW YOU CAN CREATE YOUR OWN PIECES. THE BLANK PAGES AT THE BACK ARE INTENDED FOR YOU TO SKETCH, EXPERIMENT, AND DEVELOP YOUR OWN DESIGNS, ALLOWING YOU TO BRING YOUR IDEAS TO LIFE AND REFINE YOUR STYLE. TAKE THIS SPACE TO EXPERIMENT FREELY, WITH NO LIMITATIONS OTHER THAN YOUR OWN CREATIVITY.

1.START WITH A LETTER: BEGIN BY SELECTING A LETTER FROM THE ALPHABET AS YOUR BASE. FROM THERE, GRADUALLY MODIFY AND MANIPULATE THE LETTER'S SHAPE, EXPERIMENTING WITH ANGLES, CURVES, AND EXTENSIONS. THIS METHOD ALLOWS YOU TO BUILD YOUR DESIGN ORGANICALLY WHILE MAINTAINING CONTROL OVER ITS STRUCTURE AND FLOW.

2.FOCUS ON LETTER COMPOSITION: PAY ATTENTION TO HOW LETTERS INTERACT WITH ONE ANOTHER. ENSURE THAT THEY ARE SPACED EVENLY AND THAT THEIR SIZES COMPLEMENT EACH OTHER. EXPERIMENT WITH DIFFERENT ARRANGEMENTS TO FIND A COMPOSITION THAT FEELS COHESIVE.

3.INCORPORATE FLOW: GOOD GRAFFITI OFTEN HAS A SENSE OF MOVEMENT. CONSIDER HOW THE LINES OF YOUR LETTERS CAN FLOW INTO ONE ANOTHER. USE CURVES AND ANGLES TO CREATE A DYNAMIC FEEL, GUIDING THE VIEWER'S EYE THROUGH THE PIECE.

4.ADD DEPTH WITH SHADING: ONCE YOU HAVE YOUR BASIC STRUCTURE, THINK ABOUT HOW TO ADD DEPTH. USE SHADING TECHNIQUES TO CREATE HIGHLIGHTS AND SHADOWS, GIVING YOUR LETTERS A THREE-DIMENSIONAL APPEARANCE. 5.REFINE YOUR DETAILS: AFTER ESTABLISHING THE MAIN STRUCTURE, FOCUS ON THE FINER DETAILS. ADD EMBELLISHMENTS, PATTERNS, OR TEXTURES THAT ENHANCE YOUR DESIGN WITHOUT OVERWHELMING IT. THESE DETAILS CAN ELEVATE YOUR PIECE AND MAKE IT UNIQUELY YOURS.

SHARE YOUR ART

WE ENCOURAGE YOU TO SHARE YOUR CREATIONS WITH OTHERS. JOIN THE COMMUNITIES OF FELLOW GRAFFITI ENTHUSIASTS IN THE FOLLOWING FACEBOOK GROUPS:

GRAFFITI SKETCHES: A PLATFORM TO SHARE YOUR SKETCHES AND RECEIVE CONSTRUCTIVE FEEDBACK FROM FELLOW ARTISTS.

GRAFFITI WARS: ENGAGE IN CHALLENGES AND SHOWCASE YOUR WORK ALONGSIDE OTHER TALENTED GRAFFITI ARTISTS.

SHARING YOUR ART NOT ONLY ALLOWS YOU TO CONNECT WITH OTHERS BUT ALSO HELPS YOU GROW AS AN ARTIST.